In the Company of Saints and Sinners

A True Story of Divine Rescue and Redemption

Catherine P. Butte

In the Company of Saint and Sinners

Trilogy Christian Publishers A Wholly Owned Subsidiary of Trinity Broadcasting Network

2442 Michelle Drive Tustin, CA 92780

Copyright © 2022 by Catherine P. Butte

Cover design by: Kristy Swank

For information about special discounts for bulk purchases, please contact Trilogy Christian Publishing.

Trilogy Disclaimer: The views and content expressed in this book are those of the author and may not necessarily reflect the views and doctrine of Trilogy Christian Publishing or the Trinity Broadcasting Network.

Manufactured in the United States of America

10 9 8 7 6 5 4 3 2 1

Library of Congress Cataloging-in-Publication Data is available.

ISBN: 978-1-68556-264-9

E-ISBN: 978-1-68556-265-6

Dedication

This book is dedicated to the greatest hero
I've ever known or will know,
Jesus Christ, my Lord and Savior.
Nothing and no one comes close to comparing to You.
Thank You for rescuing me over and over again.
And to my two beautiful sons, Daniel and David.
Next to Jesus and my husband, Aaron,
they are the greatest gifts of my life
and carriers of His fire and grace to the next generation.

Acknowledgments

To the Holy Spirit, my counselor and constant companion, thank You for guiding me through every step of this process from conception to completion. You deserve all the glory.

My heartfelt gratitude and deep appreciation to my husband, Aaron, for his love, prayers, and steady support—and sometimes comic relief.

And last but not least, my sincere thanks to my dear friend, Linda Love, for all her encouragement as well as her many hours of editing and counsel in preparing this manuscript to become a book. You are a treasure.

IN THE COMPANY OF SAINTS AND SINNERS:
A TRUE STORY OF DIVINE RESCUE AND REDEMPTION

TABLE OF CONTENTS

Introduction

I've been waiting about fifteen years to tell my story. If it were not for the great mercy, grace, and faithfulness of God, I would be dead. My story would have never been told. It would have died with me, but with an overflowing heart of gratitude, I am here, and I am alive and well to share my story. It could have been a story of great tragedy, but instead, I write this story redeemed, restored, and whole all because of Jesus Christ—my Redeemer. All to Him I owe.

As I wrote this book, I pictured the faces of unchurched masses reading this as a handbook for their newly-born-again lives. The greatest handbook for life will always be the Bible, but I felt I had something the Lord wanted me to share with those who will be coming to faith during the final Great Awakening. These new converts had been snatched from the fire of destruction by the sovereign hand of God and were setting out on their own adventures with the Lord. I felt this book would be an encouragement and an aid in the new life and lives they would be living in the Lord.

There are portions of this book that many may find too unimaginable or fantastic to believe. I assure you, I understand. Had I not experienced these things for myself and seen them with my own two eyes, I, too, would have had a hard time believing. The fact is I did experience these things, and because I have been a witness to them, they are a part of me. It is my sincere prayer that the Lord would open the eyes of every reader of this book to see Him and to see the truth. Instead of just taking my word for it, I hope and believe they will have their own life-changing supernatural experiences with the living God.

He can do more in a few minutes than a host of counselors, churches, and programs can do in a lifetime. Selah.

I looked and behold—I saw a white cloud, and sitting upon it was one like the Son of Man, wearing a golden crown and holding a sharp sickle. Another angel came out of the temple, shouting out to the one sitting upon the cloud, "Take your sickle and reap, for the time of reaping the harvest has come and the harvest of the earth is ripe!"

Revelation 14:14–15 (TPT)

Chapter 1: In the Beginning

In the beginning was the Word, and the Word was with God, and the Word was God. He was in the beginning with God. All things were made through Him, and without Him nothing was made that was made. In Him was life, and the life was the light of men. And the light shines in the darkness, and the darkness did not comprehend it.

John 1:1–5 (NKJV)

In my beginning with God, there was a single word. A name was spoken, and a life forever marked.

"Katie."

I heard the voice inside of me and outside of me all at the same time. It was a voice I had never heard before. It was as if time stood still for me in that moment. It was a moment I will never forget. It was a moment of destiny. My fifth-grade classroom was totally silent, and I had just sat down to take a test. It was in the silence that I heard His voice call my name. "Katie," He said. I looked up from my test to see who was calling my name. There were no other men in the room. Only my teacher and a class full of fifth graders.

Stunned, I leaned over to my nearest classmate to ask him if he had heard that voice. He looked at me and quickly said, "No." I'm not sure why I asked him that because, in my heart, I knew who was speaking the moment I heard the voice. It was God. John 10:27 (KJV) says, "My sheep hear my voice..." I heard His voice, and I knew deep within me who it was calling my name.

I sat there for a few seconds trying to process the moment the best I knew how. Supernatural encounters with God were not a part of my grid, nor was hearing the audible voice of God. I had grown up in a denominational church but knew very little about the Lord, and although my parents professed to be Christians, my upbringing was secular. I did not know God spoke to people, and I surely did not know He knew my name. But He did.

I did not realize the magnitude of that moment as a young girl about to step into my teenage years, but it was monumental. He was calling me. Twenty years later, He would call me again. This time I answered the call—I was thirty-two. I want to take you on my journey to surrender and through those lost years and out to the other side of victory.

In October 2007, on a rural Georgia farm, I had a supernatural encounter with the living God. His name is Jesus Christ. This time I heard no audible voice, but what He spoke to my heart changed my life and world forever. At the time, I was an addict, an alcoholic, and I had lost the will to live. But one encounter and one night with Him changed everything.

My real life began that night. It's really difficult to try and explain, but it was as if I woke up out of a really bad dream. The bad dream had been the thirty-two years I had lived without Him—with no real knowledge of Him. Yes, I knew He was real because of my twelve-year-old encounter, and I had other supernatural experiences that confirmed He was indeed real. But I did not *know* Him, even though He knew me. I also believe spiritual blindness was removed from my eyes so that I could actually "see." The Bible speaks of people having eyes, but they cannot see and having ears, but they cannot hear (Jeremiah 5:21). I understand. That was me before Christ.

Overnight my world seemed to turn into "technicolor," and as I look back on all the years prior to that night, it is almost like the memories are in black and white. That fateful night on a farm in 2007 was the end, and it was also the beginning. I was now a new creation in Christ. "Now, if anyone is enfolded into Christ, he has become an entirely new person. All that is related to the old order has vanished. Behold, everything is fresh and new" (2 Corinthians 5:17, TPT).

Looking back on my encounter in my fifth-grade classroom, I am now aware that I was not the only one who heard the Lord call my name. In 1 Peter 5:8, the Bible refers to us having an "adversary." Other translations call him our "great enemy." Many people just refer to him as the devil. "Stay alert! Watch out for your great enemy, the devil. He prowls around like a roaring lion, looking for someone to devour" (1 Peter 5:8, NLT).

My great enemy, the devil, also heard Him call my name. How do I know? Because of the series of attacks and storms that hit my life in the weeks, months, and years that followed. I am not ignorant of his devices or schemes today, but I was then. I did not know the Bible, and I did not have Bible-believing Christians around me to stand with me. The immediate verse following 1 Peter 5:8 says to "Stand firm against him, and be strong in your faith…" (1 Peter 5:9, NLT).

I did not have anyone around me training or teaching me spiritual truths or biblical wisdom. I had never heard that the devil was actually real and that he hated me and wanted to steal, kill, and destroy everything in my life (John 10:10). I did have a faint recollection of some biblical stories, but at that time, God wasn't real to me—not like He is now. Even after hearing His voice, I still had no idea what to do with that. I was excited and moved by the experience, but I did not know Him. Although I had been christened as a toddler and gone through "church confirmation," I wasn't born again. Jesus specifically speaks of being born again in John 3. He says, "…Before a person can even perceive God's Kingdom they must first experience a rebirth" (John 3:3, TPT).

The Bible also says in Proverbs that "God conceals the revelation of His word in the hiding place of His glory. But the honor of kings is revealed by how they thoroughly search out the deeper meaning of all that God says" (Proverbs 25:2, TPT). How I wish I would have known mature Christians at that time in my life or had strong believers around me who could have sown into my life and helped me search out the matter. How I wish I would have been born again then!

The Lord is calling young and old alike in similar experiences today, and these experiences will increase and greatly multiply with the global awakening that has already begun. We must come alongside those young in the Lord to help strengthen and increase their faith because the billion-soul harvest that is coming won't look like the church today. Many of the converts and new believers who are coming into the Kingdom will rarely have ever stepped foot in a church prior to their conversion. The Lord is literally going to snatch them out of the hand of the enemy through supernatural visitations, encounters, and a global outpouring that will change the world and the destiny of a billion souls.

That's why I'm writing this book. This book is for the harvest of souls about to come into the Kingdom and for those already in the Kingdom. This book is for the unchurched, the outcast, and "the one" called out of darkness into His marvelous light. I feel like the Lord showed me He wanted me to share my story because I am not alone in my journey—I was the unchurched, the outcast, and "the one." That is who I was—but today, I am His. The Bible actually says I am God's chosen treasure now.

> But you are God's chosen treasure—priests who are kings, a spiritual "nation" set apart as God's devoted ones. He called you out of darkness to experience His marvelous light and now He claims you as His very own. He did

this so that you would broadcast His glorious wonders throughout the world.

1 Peter 2:9 (TPT)

Most often, you hear of new-birth testimonies that include an altar call in a church, crusade, or an outreach. You also hear of young children who grow up in Christian homes being led to the Lord by their parents at young ages. I am so grateful for every born-again experience, but mine did not happen like that. My surrender and my conversion happened in my bedroom with no other person present—no one present but the Lord. This encounter in 2007 was exceptional, and it was awesome, and I had never known or heard of anyone else having anything like it prior. I did not even know something like it was possible.

Now I know that it is indeed possible, and I've heard many testimonies from others that may not be exactly like my experience but similar. I am not alone, and if you are reading this book and you have had a similar experience, you are not alone either. Our enemy may try to bring many accusations against you and create confusion around your experience, but I can testify He can't take that experience from you, and you can't ever be the same after such an experience. One thing is for sure; I was one way, and after my encounter in 2007, I was another. No one can ever take that from me. What I saw and what I experienced is mine forever, and no one will ever convince me any differently.

The twenty years between twelve and thirty-two were the desert years of my life. At the time I am writing this, I am forty-five. The absolute best years of my life are the years since that fateful night in October of 2007 when the Lord showed Himself so mighty and strong on my behalf. I have not stopped pursuing Him ever since. In a moment, He became my all-consuming fire. "...we should be extremely thankful and offer God the purest worship that delights his heart as we lay down our lives in absolute surrender, filled with awe. For our God is a holy, devouring fire!" (Hebrews 12:28–29, TPT)

So what was the result of His consuming fire in the wake of my 2007 encounter and surrender? A partial list includes getting clean and sober, as well as quitting smoking. I threw away all my antidepressants and prescription pills. I was no longer suicidal or hopeless. I had found a reason to live and was so full of hope and joy. I lost about every "friend" from my past, and most of the dysfunctional relationships were either immediately removed from life or were later removed in the years to follow. I removed myself from my old life because my old life was over. My new life had begun. It was a new beginning, and it was a glorious time for me.

I lived alone on our family farm in rural Southwest Georgia for the next two and half years of my life. I read the Bible cover to cover multiple times and began to watch hours of Christian teaching and preaching every day. I started going to church and tried to be there any time the doors were open. I fell in love for the first time in my life. No, this man wasn't like previous men I had known. This man was altogether different. He cared for my heart in a way I had never known and won me. I found Jesus Christ to be the love of my life. He proved Himself to be "the One." He was the one thing I had been searching for my entire life, and He had been there all along.

I can't say that it has always been easy. It hasn't always been easy— but it has been worth it. And where I have failed and come up short, I have always found Him to be faithful. He is faithful. The Apostle Paul writes about this in Philippians, "I pray with great faith for you, because I'm fully convinced that the One who began this gracious work in you will faithfully continue the process of maturing you until the unveiling of our Lord Jesus Christ!" (Philippians 1:6, TPT)

Please pray with me.

Lord, thank You for drawing those You have chosen to read this book. I pray for every person reading this to have eyes to see and ears to hear what You are speaking to them. I pray for revelation to flood them: spirit, soul, and body. I pray for their hearts to open to Your truth and Your love. Let them experience Your peace and presence in new and profound ways. I also pray for them to have life-changing supernatural experiences and encounters with You. We thank You and pray for the billion-soul harvest that is coming into Your Kingdom. Let Your will be done on earth as it is in heaven (Matthew 6:10). Thank You for leading these new believers to mature Christians who can love, pray with, and mentor them. Thank You for leading them to churches that preach and teach Your Word and truth without compromise—safe places where they can be planted and grow. We decree and declare Your wholeness and transformation over each of them. We rebuke the devourer and bind the enemy in their lives (Malachi 3:11). We thank You for the good work you have begun in their lives. We know that what You have begun You will also complete (Philippians 1:6). In Jesus' mighty name.

Chapter 2: The Lost Years

To fully appreciate my surrender, I feel like I should take you back to the twenty years in between "my call" when I was twelve and "my surrender" at thirty-two. Those were the "desert years" of my life—years of wondering and searching for something missing deep inside. I looked in a lot of places, trying to find what was missing. All my wondering and searching took me into some pretty dark places, and I consider these my "lost years." However, the Lord wastes nothing. I believe He has redeemed and is still in the process of redeeming these years of my life.

Shortly after hearing His audible voice when I was twelve years old, I was almost immediately hit with a false diagnosis of being dyslexic. This diagnosis put me in a special school for a time where I was "labeled" with a multitude of learning disabilities, issues, and problems. This attack went straight for my identity. The months I spent in this special school were some of the worst of my early years.

The entire time I was in this special school, I felt like I wore the label *"Something is very wrong with me."* I protested loudly every day to my parents. Finally, they agreed to get a second opinion. The next psychologist said I was not dyslexic but that I did have some learning disabilities. I was diagnosed that time as having Attention Deficient Disorder, or ADD, with hyperactivity. He saw no need to have me in a special school, and I was withdrawn. I remember rejoicing greatly and feeling like I had been released from prison.

I was thirteen the first time I drank to the point of being drunk. I loved it, and I wanted to do it again. I began sneaking beer or wine from my parents whenever I could, and within just a year or two, I was drinking and smoking with older friends on a regular basis. It became a regular part of my life from my early teens until my surrender at age thirty-two.

I had started gymnastics at the age of two and a half. I loved gymnastics as it was natural and came easy to me. I became a competitive gymnast at an early age and won my first state competition at nine. I am reminded that my coach always said I had a "God-given talent." She spoke that over me all of my years with her. She was the only coach I ever had, and she became like an adopted mother to me. For most of my preteen and early teen years, it felt like I lived at the gym, and the weekends were filled with travel to gymnastics meets all over the state.

Gymnastics became a part of my identity. It was good to feel "favored" and loved. My coach definitely favored me, and because I was winning state competitions, I had the medals and trophies to prove I was a "winner." Gymnastics was always a good outlet for all my energy, and even though I had talent, it was challenging. Gymnastics gave me goals, kept me somewhat focused, and I found a sense of accomplishment in training and winning.

At fourteen, I decided to leave competitive gymnastics. My relationship with my coach had become strained, and I was tired of training, traveling, and competing. I had also suffered a traumatic injury from a fall from the uneven bars that required surgery and rehabilitation. I was honestly never the same after that injury. Where I had once been fearless, I now found myself fearful. My confidence had been greatly shaken.

I was once willing to try anything, but now I found myself calculating the costs. Instead of "just doing it," I would look at my coach and say, "I can't" or "I'm scared." This was quite out of the ordinary for me, and it was uncomfortable. I didn't like fearing things, and I didn't like the strife I now found in the gym with my coach. I made the decision that I wasn't good enough to cut it in the "big leagues." It would be better to bow out now and begin to live a "normal" teenage life while I had the chance. So at almost fifteen, I left gymnastics. Looking back, it felt like I left my heart and a piece of myself there. Nothing and no one ever replaced or topped gymnastics in my life until I met Jesus.

As an upcoming freshman in high school, I made the decision to leave the private school I was attending to go to public school. Public school was altogether different and presented new temptations. Boys and cliques became my new thing. Boys made me feel wanted and gave me the attention I desperately desired. Cliques made me feel like I belonged, but cliques can be very deceptive. Neither boys nor cliques fulfilled any of their promises.

The boys desired physical satisfaction, and with every piece of myself I gave away, I felt more alone and isolated. The cliques desired submission, and the more I conformed to be like the group, the further I moved away from who I was divinely designed to be. Again, this was about identity. By the time I graduated high school, I did not even know who I was. I was just trying to be like everyone else—even if everyone else was lost.

There was a girl I grew up with who had given her heart to the Lord one summer at a camp she attended. I had also been to this camp, but I did not have a born-again experience there. She came back completely changed. I always knew and recognized that there was something genuinely different about her. Even though I was not ready to live the life she was living, I admired her strength and faith. To use Christian terms, "Her witness was beautiful to me." I saw something in her that was altogether lovely. She was the only born-again Christian I knew at that time. I honor her today because she is still a beautiful witness and bearing much fruit for the Kingdom on the front lines. She was one of the first people I wanted to tell after I was born again. This only confirmed what I already knew: She had made a huge impression on me.

If you are the only born-again Christian in your school, group, workplace, neighborhood, etc., please do not underestimate your influence or your witness. You may not see the fruit of your labor immediately, but you are sowing seeds. Do not conform to this world and water down your witness. It was her deliberate stand that stood out to me and made her so unique. She was sowing seed everywhere she went. Although I can't remember her ever personally witnessing to me, I do remember her life was a strong testimony that could not be ignored. Her very life preached a powerful testimony. I think Romans 12:2 (TPT) says it well, "Stop imitating the ideas and opinions of the culture around you, but be inwardly transformed by the Holy Spirit through a total reformation of how you think. This will empower you to discern God's will as you live a beautiful life, satisfying and perfect in His eyes."

In high school, I was a cheerleader, on the dance line, on the tennis team, in multiple clubs, competed and placed in beauty pageants, was chosen "Most Likely to Succeed" in my senior class, and received multiple other honors and awards but nothing satisfied. I still always felt as if something was missing, and I continued to struggle academically. School was very difficult for me, but I also stopped trying. It felt like no matter how hard I tried, it wasn't good enough, and I would still fall short. I particularly found this to be true with foreign languages. It felt as if I could not grasp learning Spanish. I actually failed it once, and when I retook it my senior year, my Spanish teacher most likely passed me so I could graduate.

Despite my mediocre grades, GPA, and SAT scores, I was "conditionally accepted" into the University of Georgia. The entrance exams I took at UGA put me in multiple remedial classes in my first quarter there, and I had to go to summer school as part of my conditional acceptance. Where I did not try in high school, I tried as hard as possible in college. I knew that if I did not perform, I could not stay. The first several quarters were very challenging, and I even had to repeat one remedial class and an English class, but I was determined. Things eventually started to shift, and my grades began to improve. I cleared all the remedial classes and found creative ways to make up the time I lost. I took full loads most summers, enrolled in independent studies, and began night school. I found night school to be a better fit because the classes were smaller, you had more interaction with the professors, and they had a reputation for being easier.

For much of my life, I had dreamed of becoming a television reporter. I even have a photo of my kindergarten graduation where I played a reporter—the "press" tab in my hat proudly displayed for all to see. In high school, I helped do morning announcements and "news" for the school. I also interviewed football players on a half-time show for our local AM radio station during football season. My heart's great desire was to now be a part of University News for the University of Georgia, graduate, and begin work as a professional reporter. To accomplish this, I would have to be accepted into the Journalism School and into the Broadcast News program. It was competitive and difficult, but I was accepted into both.

My final two years at UGA would be spent in the Journalism School, but to graduate, I would have to complete and pass multiple foreign language classes. I honestly did not know how I could do it. I did have someone suggest being tested for learning disabilities. I discovered that the University had an entire department dedicated to this and that if you were indeed found to have a learning disability, you could have your foreign language requirements substituted for other credits. I began the process and went through all the testing and was diagnosed with ADD and/or ADDHD. They also suggested that I take Ritalin to help me focus in class and study. To be honest, I was very apprehensive of taking anything, but a friend of mine had a prescription. I asked him if I could just try it and see before I got my own prescription. I took it, and it worked. I could study for hours, and I focused in class. I got my own prescription and wondered how I ever lived without it. My grades not only improved, but they skyrocketed. It felt like almost overnight, I became another person. I was hooked—literally.

With the foreign language requirements out of the way and fueled with Ritalin, I sailed through Journalism School and graduated with a Broadcast News degree. I truly felt like I had accomplished something. Three of my four grandparents were living at that time, and they were all there to see me graduate, as well as my parents. This moment in time was definitely a highlight for me during those lost years. It was made even more special that both my grandfathers and both my parents also graduated from UGA. I'm thankful for that memory and that moment in time.

During my college years, I drank very little and honestly began to detest drinking. I felt sick every time I drank. I can't help but see the hand of God in this. It's almost unexplainable why this would take place during my college years, a time when many drink more than ever. Instead, I took Ritalin and went out. Because Ritalin is a stimulant, I could stay up late, and I stayed engaged with others. I loved the way I felt on Ritalin, so I began to take more and more of it. When college was over, my Ritalin addiction followed me, and it would continue to follow me for the next decade.

I lived and worked in North Metro Atlanta as a reporter after college. I thought all my dreams would come true once I began reporting, but I hated it. I dreaded every morning going to work, and I was deeply depressed. I had to shoot, write, and edit all my stories, and I was responsible for multiple stories a day. I found the work grueling and toilsome. I did enjoy some of the human-interest stories I would occasionally get to do, but I mostly just found myself exhausted and depressed all the time. A breaking point came where I actually wondered if I was having a nervous breakdown. I could not stop crying. I cried for what seemed like days. Finally, the general manager of our station was gracious to me and gave me a few days off. I really needed it. During this time, I rested, and I began to look for a way out.

It was around this time I got engaged to someone I had been seriously dating. I would later quit my job and eventually move to the Caribbean with him so he could go to medical school on the island of St. Maarten. Technically, I could not work on the island because it was half Dutch and half French, but I volunteered and became a regular on a popular morning radio show. I lived with my then fiancé—and while I am not proud of this choice, it was the choice I made. Our choices have consequences. I thought that by running from my pain, struggles, and addictions that they would not follow me. What a joke! The Caribbean may look like paradise to some, but two dysfunctional people living together in paradise still won't make a match made in heaven.

I called off the engagement and canceled the wedding just a few weeks before our wedding date. I had to return gifts, write a lot of letters, and my parents, who were paying for the wedding, lost a great deal of money. Still, I knew it was the right thing to do. I also had a supernatural encounter during this process. It would be the first in a series of supernatural experiences I would have over the next few years—the darkest years of my life.

Please pray with me.

Lord, we thank You for never giving up on us. Thank You for pursuing us and watching over us even when we run from You and the call. Lord, I pray for every Prodigal son and daughter running right now. Help them to surrender and "come to themselves." Please bring Christians alongside them who can speak into their lives and be beautiful witnesses for You. Lord, I pray for supernatural protection and encounters with You that will reshape their thinking, change their destiny, and turn their hearts back to You. Thank You that You make all things new and can turn anything the enemy would use to harm us around for our good and Your glory (Romans 8:28). In Jesus' mighty name.

Chapter 3: The Runaway Bride

It was midday on the island of St. Maarten. I could hear the waves roll in one by one from my kitchen. I lived right on the beach. To say it was beautiful was an understatement. It was stunning. I was home all alone, and I longed to walk on the beach, one of my favorite things to do. There were so many things on my mind, and things seemed to make much better sense as I walked on the beach. As I made my way to the door, I passed by the television in the living room. Something was quietly calling me.

The Lord can use—and will use—anything He wants to speak to us. He meets us where we are. At that time in my life, I loved country music. I saw one of my favorite bands on the screen and decided to stop and turn up the music video that was playing and listen to the song.

Something powerful happened in that moment that I cannot fully explain, but it deeply touched me, changed me, and set me on a new path. It felt like everything in the room and the world went still and silent but that song. It felt like God Himself was speaking to me. It was not scary, and it was not weird. I felt deeply loved and known. I felt like He was speaking a very clear message to me.

In the natural, I was listening to a love song, but I was having something very supernatural happen as well. It is hard to convey in human terms what was spoken to my heart in that encounter, but I mostly felt His love. I also had a "knowing" that my engagement and the person I was engaged to were not love. In fact, I felt like I was shown it would lead only to loss and pain. If I could have been honest with myself, I already knew this. Deep in my heart, I knew we didn't really love each other, and from the beginning, this relationship had been difficult and painful.

The Lord spoke hope and love to my heart by showing me true love was possible, and He showed me that true love was waiting for me. When the encounter in my home was over, I went to the beach and walked with Him. No, I could not see Him, but now that I know Him, I can look back and tell you that I walked with the living God that day. When our walk was over, I knew I had to call off my wedding. I was supernaturally filled with the strength, courage, and faith to do it. It was a very good decision.

The beautiful wedding gown I would have worn was put in storage, and the grand party we had planned was canceled, but what the Lord had shown me on that beach and whispered to my heart in a love song would come to pass. It didn't take place when I thought it would or how I thought it would, but I would find true love, and nothing comes close to comparing.

I packed up my belongings and left the island. Leaving wasn't easy. I had fallen in love with St. Maarten and the Caribbean. I also had come to love the people. I will never forget one of the greatest lessons I learned there. I saw the love, peace, and happiness so many of the island's poorest people seemed to possess. The dichotomy of the poverty of many of the locals and the stark contrast of mega-wealthy coming in on massive yachts was obvious. But what I saw and couldn't ignore was so much joy and happiness, even among the poorest locals on the island. I didn't see the same happiness on the wealthy people I knew or the mega-rich visiting the island. I began to seriously contemplate this in my heart while on the island and after I left.

I think a lot of things were going through my mind as the wheels came up and the jet took off the day I left St. Maarten. I knew "island life" was now in the past, and that was sad, but I was headed back home to the US, and that made me happy and hopeful. I thought I would make a brand-new start, and I wanted to believe that was possible, but I was still dragging my past, pain, and addictions along with me. A new start would not be possible without making real changes in my life, but that was a lesson I was still in the process of learning.

Meanwhile, my addiction to prescription stimulants had spiraled out of control. I had long since stopped Ritalin and began taking more powerful stimulants like Adderall and Dexedrine. I was taking double, triple, or more of the amount I was prescribed of Dexedrine in one dose. I was staying up for days sometimes and then taking medications to calm me down and help me sleep. These new "calming" medications were also highly addictive. I was taking pills to get up and taking pills to sleep.

When I returned to the States, I began to look for a job as a reporter. I had experienced some success in the Caribbean in broadcasting. I really did like working on the morning radio show. I had taken over the news in the mornings, and people seemed to like the change I brought. When I was leaving the island, the owner of the station asked me to stay. He wanted to expand the news department and offered to make me the head of it. I seriously considered his offer, especially since I had grown to love St. Maarten and the people there so much, but something told me that if I did not leave then, I would never leave. This was more than just a "feeling." This was more like a "knowing in my heart." I didn't fully understand it, but I felt I had no choice but to leave the island.

Back in the States, I adjusted as best I could, but it was an extremely dark time for me. I was still cleaning up the canceled wedding; I was trying to find a job, and my addictions were still controlling my life. I was hurting. I "slapped some band-aids on" and pretended I was fine. I was not fine. I was a mess. Instead of finding a job, I needed to find help. I needed full-time rehabilitation at this point, but I did not get it, and I did not want it. I wanted to pretend and believe that somehow it was all just going to be okay.

I did eventually find a job. I was hired as a reporter for a station in Rock Hill, SC, just outside of Charlotte, NC. I moved, and all my past, pain, addictions, and struggles moved with me. I thought it would be a new beginning, but it was not. I did enjoy reporting there more. I had a cameraman and an editor to help. It was not as stressful, my salary was better, and it was also a better working environment—but I was not better.

I was also now in an extremely dysfunctional relationship with an older man who had greater addictions than me. To make matters worse, I was now taking ecstasy and other street drugs on a regular basis. It felt like my life was completely spiraling out of any sort of control. I was trying to keep up at work and on camera as if I had it all together, but when I wasn't working, I was either high or wanted to get high. I was an addict. And although I could not bring myself to admit that at the time, as I look back, I am still amazed at my own level of gross deception.

Within a year of starting my job in South Carolina, I quit. In my heart, I also walked away from journalism and reporting forever. I was walking out a painful cycle of defeat and destruction, and I did not know how to escape. This would have been a really great time for me to seek out treatment and rehabilitation for my addictions, but it would have been an even better time to turn my life and everything in it over to the Lord. It truly reminds me of the scriptures where people have "eyes but cannot see," and they have "ears but cannot hear."

"Listen, you foolish and senseless people, with eyes that do not see and ears that do not hear" (Jeremiah 5:21, NLT).

When you hear what I say, you will not understand.
When you see what I do, you will not comprehend. For
the hearts of these people are hardened, and their ears
cannot hear, and they have closed their eyes—so their
eyes cannot see, and their ears cannot hear, and their
hearts cannot understand, and they cannot turn to me
and let me heal them.

Matthew 13:14–15 (NLT)

I am still baffled as I look back and realize that it never even
occurred to me to go to church. I think at the time, my idea of church
was the denominational church I attended as a child. I saw in my
mind the steeple, the stained glass, the pews, and the minister in a
gown. I had never seen His power there or seen His Spirit move there.
To my knowledge, I also never heard the gospel message there, nor
can I remember ever feeling His presence as a child, teen, or adult.

I had put God in a box, and I now know that He doesn't fit
well in boxes. I was totally ignorant of the fact that God is not
confined to denominations, grand churches, or the four walls
of a church. As a then addict, I didn't think "my idea" of church
would help me. This deeply saddens me. Today, I cannot imagine
my life without His presence. I also cannot imagine going to a
church where His Spirit does not move and there is no power. I
serve a powerful God! I have seen Him move powerfully in my
life. I have seen Him supernaturally break chains of addiction and
bondage in my life, and I have witnessed Him do it for others. I
have seen things in church that left me totally speechless, and I
have seen things in revival that bewildered my mind and my eyes.

Right now, there are multitudes who know nothing of the power,
goodness, and love of God. They have either put Him in their box,

written Him off, or most likely have never experienced Him to know He is real and wants to move powerfully for them. They are ignorant of God.

Ignorant (adjective): "Lacking in knowledge or training; unlearned. Lacking knowledge or information as to a particular subject or fact. Uninformed; unaware. Due to or showing lack of knowledge or training."[1]

I was totally ignorant of God, and the results were devastating. It didn't dawn on me that "church" could help. I was right. Church as I knew it probably would not have helped me, but Jesus—He changes everything. I still had not cried out to Jesus. I still had not surrendered my life nor answered the call that I had received when I was twelve years old. At the time, I was twenty-five.

I've heard it said that "ignorance is bliss." Nothing could be further from the truth. The Bible says, "It is the truth that sets a person free" (John 8:32). It also says, "My people perish for lack of knowledge" (Hosea 4:6).

Maybe you are also ignorant of God or the things of God. Maybe you have never been to church, or you've had a bad experience in church. Maybe you have just put God in a box. Whatever your past experience and wherever you are right now, the Lord wants to meet you where you are and help you. You are not alone.

1   "Ignorant," Dictionary.com, https://www.dictionary.com/browse/ignorant.

Please pray with me.

Lord, we thank You that You meet us where we are and You are here in this moment with us. Thank You for not letting us stay where we are but leading us to greater truth, greater freedom, and a greater revelation of You and Your great love for us. Please forgive us for putting limits on You and placing You in our own boxes. You are the creator of the universe. You spoke and created everything. You breathed Your life in each one of us, and no one knows us better than You. You are all-powerful and omniscient. Lord, we pray You would open our eyes to see You and give us ears to hear You. Thank You for breaking any chains of addiction and deception off of us and leading us to lasting freedom and true breakthrough in each of our lives. In Jesus' mighty name. Amen.

> And may you also have the power to understand, as all God's people should, how wide, how long, how high, and how deep His love is. May you experience the love of Christ, though it is too great to understand fully. Then you will be made complete with all the fullness of life and power that comes from God.
>
> Ephesians 3:18–19 (NLT)

Chapter 4: Chaos in the Capitol

In the spring of 2001, I moved to Washington, DC. I found an apartment on Capitol Hill and moved in, hoping to find a job in politics. Despite all the dysfunction and addiction in my life, I was able to find a great job. I had friends and family who lived and worked on Capitol Hill, and they introduced me to a lot of new people. I also met a young lobbyist who I began to date. It seemed like almost instantly, I had found a new life, new job, new friends, and what looked like a promising new relationship.

This is the cycle you can see repeated in my life over and over: A bright new beginning with what looks like endless possibilities and the cycle of defeat and self-destruction left in its wake. Sadly, Washington, DC, would prove to be no different. I had only lived in DC a few months and was up getting dressed to go to work on a beautiful September morning when the unbelievable happened. I always got dressed watching the morning news. Suddenly, they broke in with breaking news that a plane had crashed into one of the Twin Towers. The morning of 9/11 had begun.

I watched with my roommates in horror as the events of that day unfolded. We waited in silence as rumors of other jets possibly headed to Washington or even the Capitol building circled on the different news networks. We watched as the Pentagon was hit and saw both towers crumble to the ground. It felt like that day lasted forever.

While work and life resumed in Washington, life looked very different after 9/11. There was a heavy military presence in the city and around it. There were also the 2001 anthrax attacks that took place after 9/11 in Washington and other cities. These took place just blocks from my home and work. It felt as though everyone was living on edge for months. Meanwhile, my addictions only seemed to grow worse in an environment so full of fear, uncertainty, and even death. I was now addicted to Klonopin and Xanax. These drugs are similar to tranquilizers or Valium and have a calming effect on nerves. While I had originally taken them to help me sleep, I was now taking them all the time and drinking as I did. These meds and alcohol were now my drugs of choice.

I began to have blackouts, and I wanted to stop taking the pills, but I couldn't. This class of medication has to be gradually decreased, and the process of detoxing and withdrawal can be severe. I knew I couldn't do it on my own, so I spoke with my doctor and went through a medical detox. I was actually getting help, and for the first time in years, I was clean from prescription pills. I felt like I had actually accomplished something, and I had. Detoxing was painful and difficult, but I wanted to be free. Sadly, this freedom did not last long. I began taking stimulants again, and the cycle of addiction continued. It wasn't long after starting the stimulants again that I realized I needed the tranquilizers, and the vicious cycle resumed.

Around this time, my boyfriend and I broke up, and I spiraled into a deep abyss of depression, despair, and worsening addiction. I stopped eating, and I lost a lot of weight. I looked terrible, and where I was sort of able to pull off being a "functioning addict" in the past, now I was having a difficult time faking it. I met a friend who had a background in retail, and our friendship became centered around shopping in Georgetown. We began to dream together of starting our own business and retail store. We both felt we had some capital to invest in the venture and began to write a business plan. We often stayed up all night fueled by Dexedrine and then went to work during the day.

We found a vacant storefront on Wisconsin Avenue in Georgetown and began to step out and pursue our dream. I eventually quit my job on Capitol Hill and began to throw myself and everything I could into opening our new retail store. I moved out of my apartment on Capitol Hill and moved into a second-story apartment in the heart of Georgetown, just two blocks from our new storefront. When my friend and business partner failed to come up with her part of the capital for the business, we hit a major roadblock. Just weeks prior to our grand opening, our friendship dissolved as well as our partnership. I was now in it alone, carrying the sole responsibility of everything. At times I thought I would simply be crushed under the weight of it all.

I already had possession of the storefront and was still moving in and making renovations when I had one of the first in a series of supernatural encounters that would greatly impact my life. My store was next to a French bakery and restaurant. Overwhelmed, exhausted, and hungry, I went next door for lemonade and a brie sandwich and sat down to eat in the restaurant. I was at a table for two, and my seat was facing the door. I could see a woman walking directly to me from across the room, and as she approached my table, the entire room went silent, and everything around me looked blurry or almost out of focus—everything but her.

As she approached, I could see her and hear her with perfect clarity. She asked if she could sit down with me, and I said, "Yes." I had let this woman in my store earlier that day. She had knocked and asked if she could take a look. Reluctantly, I had let her in, despite being closed and rushing to complete everything for our grand opening. Later, I discovered she had even signed the guestbook I put in the store. She signed it "Mary Bush."

As this woman began to sit, I was engulfed and undone by the weight of the moment. Just seconds before, I was sitting in the middle of a bustling, busy French café full of people; now, the restaurant was silent, and I could only see and hear this woman. As she sat down and my eyes connected with hers, I again found myself undone. I felt like I was looking directly into the eyes of love, and a tangible peace came over me that I had never known or experienced before that moment.

There was no "small talk" or reintroductions. She simply asked me, "Have you ever known what it is like to be unconditionally loved?" I'm not sure how long it took me to answer. I was still trying to process those eyes I was looking into. There was love pouring from them directly into me, and I remember thinking to myself, *Am I looking into the eyes of God Himself?*

I wondered to myself, *What is happening here?* I had no grid for this, and at the time, I had no biblical foundation, theology, or Bible college training to help. This was totally uncharted waters for me.

I began to answer by telling her about my great-grandmother. She was the closest thing I had ever known to unconditional love. I was born on her birthday and named after her, and she greatly favored me. She made me feel deeply loved and truly special over and over again. I missed her. She died my freshman year in college. She left me her engagement ring, and to this day, I wear it as my own.

"Mary Bush" listened as I shared about my great-grandmother, and when I was done, she spoke again. She said, "You need to know that you are deeply loved and watched over." Then she repeated herself, "You need to know that you are very watched over." I can hear these words in my heart right now as if it had just happened. I will never forget the weight of those words and the love that flooded me as I heard them. Then she said, "You need to know that everything is going to be okay." Again, I was flooded with peace and a knowing in my heart that it would be just as she had said it. Everything was going to be okay! So much was said during that time, and so few words were used. She got up, and I watched her walk across the room and leave out the front door. The room and everything in it went back to normal.

I remember just sitting there for what felt like forever, stunned and even dazed by what had just happened. *What did just happen?* I thought. *Was that an angel? Those eyes... I will never forget those eyes. How do I get up from this table when it feels as if the world stopped spinning while I sat here? What am I supposed to do with what I just experienced?* These were some of the thoughts I had, but I mostly just had a knowing in my heart that things were never going to be "normal" for me again. I was right.

It was the summer of 2002 when this happened. As I write this book, it is the summer of 2021. Almost twenty years have passed since that fateful day, but I remember it all as if it happened yesterday. In the twenty years since then, I finally surrendered my life to Christ and began the most exciting and amazing journey of my life with Him. But on that summer day in Georgetown, I was unaware of Scripture and ignorant of the things of God.

Hebrews 13:2 (TPT) says, "And show hospitality to strangers, for they may be angels from God showing up as your guests."

Hebrews 1:14 (TPT) says, "What role then, do the angels have? The angels are spirit-messengers sent by God to serve those who are going to be saved."

Was that an angel? The honest answer is, "I do not know for sure." For years after, I was certain it had to be an angel; however, after I got saved, I wondered if that was actually the truth. Once I began to move in the things of God, see Him move through others, and learned about the gifts of the Spirit, I realized that "Mary Bush" may very well have been a highly anointed Christian who simply followed the leading of the Holy Spirit and was used powerfully. Either way, the events that day helped to pave the way for my eventual salvation, and it gave me great hope. I would need that hope in the months and years that would follow because it was about to get increasingly darker and more difficult.

My store opened, and it was successful. People seemed to like it, and I was busy. I sold unique items and specialized in handmade and one-of-a-kind creations. I also had a baby section in the store and sold high-end baby items that were beautiful and distinctive. There was a baby boom going on in DC at the time. It was about a year after 9/11. People flooded the store to see the baby section. The store was even featured on the front page of *The Washington Post* business section.

After being featured in *The Post*, the store was also mentioned and seen in several other national magazines. The good press continued locally as well. We were featured in many local Washington publications, and I found myself busier than ever. Despite having employees, I was working night and day to keep up, literally. I took pills to stay up and work for days, and then I would crash and sleep for days. I didn't know how to manage my business, and I didn't know how to manage my life.

Within a year at my first location, the decision was made to move to a more prime retail location directly in the heart of Georgetown. The new location was undoubtedly impressive, but the move to put us there felt as if it would nearly take me out. I was now in a much higher profile location as well as a larger location. I would also eventually need private security and went from barely managing a few employees to having more than I knew what to do with. I was not just stretched thin; I was grossly overwhelmed and in over my head. I mishandled a lot of things; I mistreated a lot of people, and I made a boatload of mistakes.

I finally reached a breaking point when I could not pull myself out of bed and could not work. I didn't even want to take pills to do it. I just wanted out. The decision was made to close the store. I slept for a week or more while my store was packed up and everything was put in storage. The store was closed, and the dream was over. I was both heartbroken and relieved.

I spent the next few months floundering in the wake of failure. I had no business, no job, and no prospects of a job. I had a list of failures and addictions that were stacking up, and I was still having to deal with the financial mess and fallout from the business. I was disappointed and depressed, but I was also glad to be relieved of the pressure. Around that time, I began seeing the lobbyist I had started dating when I first moved to Washington. In time, we began to date seriously. We eventually would get engaged, but our engagement was really over before it even started.

I was doing all the same things and expecting different results. I brought all my addictions and issues into the engagement, and he brought his. I had been heartbroken by our breakup years earlier and never moved on during all that time. I had always hoped we would get back together, but now that we were back together, I wondered what I was really thinking.

We called off the engagement, and I decided to move back to my home state of Georgia. I was thirty years old. I had moved to Washington when I was twenty-five and had seen a lot in those few years. I had seen some highs and felt the weight of crushing lows. I had seen some success and had known failure. Now, I was stepping into what would be the final battle over the salvation of my soul. If it sounds dramatic, that's because it was. As I left Washington, I had no idea I was headed into the battle of my life. I did not know that there was a spiritual war being waged for my life and destiny. What a shame to be so ignorant!

"Your hand-to-hand combat is not with human beings, but with the highest principalities and authorities operating in rebellion under the heavenly realms. For they are a powerful class of demon-gods and evil spirits that hold this dark world in bondage" (Ephesians 6:12, TPT).

The battles that had played out in Washington were child's play compared to the showdowns that would unfold over the next year and a half. It would be the most difficult time of my life. It was not just dark; at times, it felt as if gross darkness was overtaking me. There would be moments where I felt as if I was looking at death right in the face. In fact, I did look at death in the face, but death lost. The devil didn't take me out. I'm still here.

"For behold, the darkness shall cover the earth, And deep darkness the people; But the Lord will arise over you, and His glory will be soon upon you" (Isaiah 60:2, NKJV).

I would not wish what happened to me during those final months on anyone, but looking back, I am grateful—not for the experience but for the result. Everything the enemy intended for evil the Lord has turned around for my good (Genesis 50:20). Not only did I give my life to Christ, but the Lord has been restoring, redeeming, and resurrecting my life ever since. When I stepped out of the darkness and into His marvelous light, everything changed (1 Peter 2:9). The dysfunction, the destructive cycles of self-defeat, the addict and the alcoholic you've been reading about, well, that's not me anymore. That person died. I was reborn in a moment (John 3:3). I'm not who I was. I'm a new creation in Christ (2 Corinthians 5:17).

I may not be proud of the things I did, and I'm not proud, but I'm also not guilty anymore. Jesus Christ bore my dysfunction, depression, addiction, sickness, shame, and all my sin on the cross two thousand years ago. Today, I stand redeemed and restored by His amazing grace. He has given me His righteousness and His holiness and a totally new future and destiny. He is hope, and if you are reading this book, He wants to do the exact same for you.

Please pray with me.

Lord, I thank You for mercy. You are so merciful. Thank You that we do not get what we deserve, but instead, You show us unfailing love and mercy. Lord, we cry out for mercy. Please forgive us, Lord. Help us to surrender to You fully and live in a place of full surrender all the time. Where we have missed the mark, either in ignorance or willfully, help us to get back on track. Please give us wisdom and greater understanding and increase our discernment. Thank You for making all things new in our lives. In Jesus' mighty name. Amen.

Chapter 5: The Beginning of the End

"Hurry up, Beazy! Quickly, Bogey," I said to my two bichons frises. It was winter as I stood outside my condo in Atlanta, Georgia, letting my pups do their business. Even though it was night, the light from the city and the towering buildings around me glowed. I wasn't in Washington anymore, and if I can be honest, I had a bad feeling about my move to Atlanta from the start. I was living in Midtown Atlanta at the time and hoping to find another job in politics.

Beazy was a gift given to me by a Jewish attorney I had dated while I lived in Georgetown. He was much older than me, born and raised in New York City, and seemed to think that a puppy would be the perfect Valentine's gift. Reluctantly, I agreed. Beazy was one of the best things that ever happened to me, although things were tough for Beazy during our first years together. I failed him too, over and over.

Because Beazy was alone for long periods of time, I thought that he would do better with a companion, and so "Bogey" joined the journey. I had both dogs before I left Washington, so they were now with me in Atlanta. These two gifts from God were with me through the darkest days and also through the best and brightest of new beginnings.

Even though Atlanta was much closer to my hometown in South Georgia, I missed Washington. Atlanta didn't feel like home, and I kept waiting for this to eventually change. I thought if I just found the right friends or made some adjustments, I would like it better, but that never really changed. I did eventually move from Midtown to a loft in Buckhead. Midtown is located between downtown Atlanta to the south and an area known as "Buckhead" to the north. While I did like it better in Buckhead, it was a bad choice to live within walking distance of so many bars.

It was around this time that I was out with some friends, and I was pulled over and arrested for DUI. I spent the better part of the night in the Fulton County Jail locked up. When I was finally released, my friends picked me up. I will never forget the song that was playing in my friend's SUV as we drove away from the jail. It was "Jesus Take the Wheel" by Carrie Underwood. We all had a good laugh, but there was really nothing funny about it.

They had no idea that the Lord had been pursuing me for the past twenty years. They had no clue what that song did to my heart when I heard it. They did not know that a song could or would convict me so deeply. Yes, I may have been laughing on the outside, but I was crying inside. Indeed, it was time for Jesus to take the wheel.

With the help of an attorney, I was eventually able to get the charge reduced to "reckless driving," but I would have to meet with a probation officer regularly and perform community service. The community service had to be performed within a year, and I would have to meet with a probation officer during that time. It was also around that time that I finally found a job. I was hired as a lobbyist, and I would be working for a small firm with a list of powerful and influential clients. The small firm just had two lobbyists, and I was working directly for them and with them. I was hired in the summer of 2006, and at first, I truly loved it.

I went to a lot of dinners, met a lot of people, drank a lot of wine, and found myself right in the middle of some of the biggest political players in the state. It was all going pretty well when we went to an overnight convention about an hour south of Atlanta. It was early fall, and I had only been with the firm a few months. After the afternoon and evening events were over, a group of us had decided to continue the night at a local bar. An elected official was with us that night and he also had a law enforcement escort and a state Suburban. We all rode together in his vehicle and spent the rest of the night drinking at a bar before heading back to our hotel.

This elected official was good friends with both the men I worked with. He also had been drinking heavily that night. We all went back to the hotel together in his SUV. When we arrived at the hotel at the end of the night, I noticed this man was now with another young female lobbyist. I did not remember seeing her at the bar, and I did not know her name, but I knew she was a lobbyist because I recognized her from the capitol. I also knew this man was married and that this was not his wife. He and the young female lobbyist went into his hotel room and closed the door. I was left in the hallway with the others, and we all went to our own rooms and slept the remainder of the night. It was pretty obvious what had taken place. I had no plans to discuss it with anyone, and I intended to mind my own business. We all got up the next morning and went back to Atlanta.

The following weekend I traveled with one of our partners to the University of Georgia for a home football game where we had been invited into the president's box. The elected official from the previous weekend was in the box, and so was his law enforcement escort. The escort began to talk with me, and we laughed and spoke briefly about the previous weekend at the convention. He then looked at me and said, "You know nothing happened with that lobbyist and (he named the man I am intentionally not naming) that night." I looked at him and had no idea what he was talking about. What did he mean "nothing happened"? We all saw them together, and it was very obvious that there was a lot going on. Then we saw them go into his hotel room and not come out. What did he mean "nothing happened"?

This is the point where I found myself on the wrong side of ignorance again. When he told me that "nothing happened," I looked at him and laughed. I said, "We both know what happened."

Looking back, I often wonder how things could or would have played out differently had I given another answer.

On October 27, 2006, I got up and went to work like any other day, but this day was different. For about a decade, I referred to this day as "the worst day of my life." I don't call it that anymore. This was the beginning of the end. This was the day when everything changed, and nothing would ever be the same in its wake.

I was supposed to be meeting the men I worked for at a private club in Buckhead. It was located at the top of a skyrise right in the center of Buckhead. I sat in the lobby of the club, waiting for either one of the lobbyists I worked for to arrive, but they were not there, and I had no word via text or email where they were. Meanwhile, I waited. This was very unusual. Not only that neither one wouldn't be there, but also that I would have no word as to why they were late. I started to wonder if they were coming. Around the same time, I noticed what seemed like a deluge of men all dressed the same with briefcases walking in and out. I had the strangest and almost alarming feeling about these men as they walked around and about me.

For a few days, I had been noticing the same vehicles parking outside my condo and following me as I would leave. I wanted to dismiss it as just my mind playing games on me, but I was pretty sure I was intentionally being followed. Now I sat in a lobby alone in a private club with a really strange scene unfolding around me.

I worked as a lobbyist in the state capitol and was around men in suits with briefcases all the time. This was different. This was mechanical, organized, and intimidating. I was starting to get frightened. I'm not sure how long I waited there, but I eventually began to listen to my instincts. I had no proof, but something told me I was being set up. I felt in that moment if I did not leave, then it would be disastrous.

I jumped up and walked as quickly as I could to the elevators. When I got up to go, I was sure I was being followed, and when I got to the lobby of the building on the ground floor, I was scared to go to my car alone because it was parked in the parking garage. I did not think that was a safe place to go. Quickly, I thought if I ran on foot out of the building and out into the open, that would be the safest place for me to go, and I would have the best chance of escape.

I ran for some time and finally made it into a small nearby shop for refuge and asked for help. I didn't think these men would follow me into a small business, and they didn't. While I was in this small store, I decided it would be best to try and get to my doctor's office nearby. His office was the closest public place where I actually knew someone who might be able to help. It was a few miles down the road, but if I could jump on a bus, I could get there quickly. I felt he would be a safe person to turn to if he would believe me. This doctor was actually a psychiatrist, and he was prescribing me the various medications I was taking and addicted to.

I ran from the small business and straight to a bus on the main street. This time I did not see anyone following me or that I recognized from earlier. I caught a bus to my doctor's office and told the receptionist it was an emergency. I waited until he could see me and then told him every detail of what had taken place over the last few days and that morning. I understand that telling this story to a psychiatrist wasn't the best idea, but I felt I had no other recourse. I was scared, and I literally felt I was running for my life.

In short, he wanted me to stop taking the stimulants because he thought they had brought on this "episode," and he wanted me to immediately take high-powered antipsychotics. I did as he said, and I remember the "numbing" effect that began almost immediately. It made me feel like a zombie. He was kind enough to drive me home since I had no vehicle. He told me to get some sleep and to rest for a few days.

I did sleep. I slept for a long time, and I wanted to wake up to a new reality. That did not happen. What I had experienced was not a bad dream or a psychotic episode, and no amount of prescription medication could undo what I had seen and experienced. It was real, and I do understand it may sound far-fetched, but I assure you it happened. I also learned a lesson from that day. I now felt that if I were to tell anyone the real truth, I would be counted as "crazy," and possibly more drastic measures would be taken. Specifically, I feared that if I said anything more about what happened as if it were real, I would possibly be put in a hospital or worse. I felt hopelessly trapped.

I stopped taking the powerful medication, and I went back to work as if nothing had happened. I think I hoped in my heart that if I pretended it didn't happen, maybe whatever happened would just magically stop. It did not stop, and it only got worse. I had a BlackBerry phone at that time in 2006. I felt my phone calls were monitored; I felt my emails were being read, and I felt my phone was being used to actually listen in on my life. How did I know all this? My phone would do weird things and seemed to take on a life of its own at times. I was being followed in my car, followed at the capitol, and followed wherever I went. For this to be taking place on such a grand scale, I knew I was being tracked somehow, and I just assumed it was probably my phone, so I got a new one. That didn't help.

I also felt my life was in danger. One day as I left my condo, I heard a door open down the hall from me and clearly heard the steps of someone walking my way. The floors were concrete, so you could hear every step, but because the hallway turned, I could not see the person. I could only hear them coming. The next thing I heard was a gun being cocked. I know little about guns and even less about them being cocked, but I have seen enough movies to know what it sounds like. I literally could hear every step of a person walking my way with hard-soled shoes, and then I heard the sound of a gun being cocked. I quickly went back to my door, closed, and locked it. Nothing more happened that day, but I got the message. I'm not sure if they really wanted me dead or if they just wanted me to think that, but no matter, I feared for my life greatly.

I always went back to wondering what I had stumbled into that would cause or justify any of the things that were taking place. It felt like I was living in a bad Hollywood movie that never ended. I was researching online and combing through news articles, trying to find anything that would help me understand what would have caused this great uproar. I still do not know what really happened and why. I can only tell you what happened to me and what I witnessed.

I went to the Atlanta Police Department and filed a complaint. I never heard anything more about it. I tried to file an ethics complaint at the capitol while I was still a lobbyist, but as I sat down to file the complaint, my BlackBerry went off with an emergency text from my boss. I would have to come back to complete it. I never made it back because that was one of my last days as a lobbyist. I even drove to one of Atlanta's major news stations and asked to speak with one of their investigative reporters who I knew covered politics. I waited in the lobby, but eventually, I was told he wasn't there. I had run out of all my options for anyone I felt I could turn to.

In the meantime, the intimidation tactics were growing more intense daily. These were not just simply in "my head." I was being followed and stalked twenty-four seven. I went to a dinner once with a friend and got up to go to the restroom, and the men who were following me were so bold as to literally block me from going to the restroom. Three or four of them stood in a line across the pathway and would not let me cross. I looked at them and literally asked them to please move out of my way. They did finally move, but the message was clear: "We are here, and we aren't going anywhere."

It's one thing to be in a loud, crowded restaurant full of people and have that happen, but I was a single young woman who lived alone. It was scary to be alone knowing you were being followed and watched. I had become almost too frightened to take my dogs out day or night; however, when I did take them out, I became aware of a man with a dog who would often stand watch at the entrance of the building.

I would have to walk through the parking garage to go out to the wooded area behind our condos. I would take Beazy and Bogey out there, but it was wooded and dark, and it really wasn't a very safe place under normal conditions. Still, my pups needed to go out, and I often saw this man standing there when I would take them. He always just stood with his dog and just watched me. I wasn't afraid of this man. In fact, I had a great deal of peace every time I saw him. He had normal clothes on and was very relaxed. I knew or recognized almost everyone who lived in our building, but I did not know this man. I had never seen him park his car, passed him in the lobby, or run into him on the elevator. I only would see him when I took my dogs out, and he would only be there long enough to watch me until I would start to come back inside. Then he would be gone.

The man had dark hair and was tall. He looked to be in good shape, and he had a large dog with him on a leash. I was so grateful for him and his dog. It felt like I had an ally and that someone was actually watching over me. For a few moments with him around, I felt as if I wasn't by myself in this lonely fight. I never spoke to this man. I only came to know and appreciate him from afar. Who was this man who appeared and seemingly disappeared almost every time I took my dogs out?

The beautiful words from the fateful lunch in Georgetown with "Mary Bush" would come to mind. "Never forget how watched over you are. It is all going to be okay."

On what would end up being one of my final days at the capitol, I was given a package by one of my bosses to deliver to someone in the capitol. But in the process of all the drama, I actually set it down on a bench and left it.

I realized pretty quickly what I had done and began to retrace my steps in the capitol to find the package. It was gone. I made every attempt to find it and reached out to security for help, but the package was gone. I was devastated, as this was yet another failure on my part.

I went home after work and took Beazy and Bogey out. I walked through the garage and then behind my condo and let them out and returned the exact same way. When I came back through the garage, the package I had lost in the capitol was sitting on top of my neighbor's car. It was in plain sight, and it was there because whoever put it there knew I would walk right past that car and see it.

I didn't touch the package. Instead, I went straight to the front desk and asked for the surveillance footage of the garage. I knew they were recording all the activity in the garage for safety reasons, and I knew whoever put that package there had done it only moments earlier. It was not there when I walked past that car on my way out, but it was there when I came walking back through.

The front desk manager said he was not authorized to release the footage, and I tried to explain to him what happened, but he wouldn't budge. Overwhelmed and completely frustrated, I went to my condo with a new resolve. I packed my bags and my dogs and left for my family's home in the North Carolina mountains. I felt sure I could decompress and maybe outrun whatever was following me if

I could get there. It was a beautiful mountain home just two short hours away. I left Atlanta and headed for higher ground.

Running from the battle isn't the answer, but sometimes a strategic retreat is wisdom. When I got to the mountains, I did find refuge there. I was traumatized, and I was carrying that trauma with me. It was now February, and I had been living in fear and trembling for months, but it felt like a lifetime. In the mountains during the winter, there are so few people around, and it felt like another world compared to the reality I had been living in. I bought some groceries, built a lot of fires, and rested. I found the company of Beazy and Bogey to be so comforting. As far as I could tell, I also never noticed or saw anyone following me while I was there, and I was not aware of being watched. *I could get used to this*, I thought.

Getting away from everything that was taking place was probably the very best thing I could have done. I was able to get a better perspective and realize I could not go on this way. While I was in North Carolina, I got an email from the partners of the firm. They fired me. I was relieved, and I thought things might be over, but they were not. When I finally went back to Atlanta, the battle I had run from was waiting for me.

During the following weeks in Atlanta, things did not get better. I still feared for my life, and I was traumatized by all that had happened to me. I was drinking heavily, taking prescription pills, and crying myself to sleep at night. I was scared to leave my condo, and for weeks, I lived there barricaded—leaving only if I absolutely had no choice. My parents asked me to come home. I grew up in a small town about four hours south of where I lived in Atlanta. I decided to go, and I packed up my things and my dogs and drove south. I was so fearful and traumatized, but at the same time, I still had a resolve deep in my heart that everything would somehow be okay.

While at my parents' home, there was a knock on the door as I sat in the den watching TV. The next thing I knew, local law enforcement officers were in the room with me. They were there to take me back to Atlanta for treatment. My parents had obtained an order to have me taken to treatment against my will. I didn't say much. I had so little fight left in me. I just got in the back of the patrol car and made the four-hour trip back to Atlanta.

I was taken to an inpatient rehabilitation center in Atlanta. I spent the first few weeks detoxing from Klonopin, which was excruciating. They forced me to take antipsychotics, which never removed the reality of what I had actually been through but did produce unbearable side effects. I eventually stopped taking these antipsychotics and would flush them down the toilet. I began going to AA meetings, and being clean and sober was good, but behavior modification without a real heart change is just a "temporary fix." I was released after about six weeks of treatment to go back home with my parents.

While I was in treatment, my family moved me out of my condo in Atlanta. I was thirty-one and moving back in with my parents. I had no job and no home of my own, and I could now add "involuntary hospitalization" to my growing list of achievements. To say I felt like a failure is an understatement, but some good things did come out of rehab.

I was required by law to complete community service and a state drug and alcohol awareness class because of my reckless driving offense. I had not done either, and if I had not completed them in Atlanta during a period of time, I would most likely be put in jail. With the crisis of all that took place from October of 2006 through the following spring, I did not complete it. When I was placed in treatment, I was given an extension to complete these requirements without jail time. For that, I am very grateful. I can only see the hand of God and His mercy in this.

I was released from rehab in the summer of 2007. I completed the alcohol and drug class in my hometown and also fulfilled my community service at a local Christian ministry that ministered to young children and teens. It was at that ministry I would later come back and work after my conversion. The leadership of that ministry saw firsthand the "before and after" of my testimony.

I was also reunited with Beazy and Bogey. They had both been taken to a farm where they had lived during the time I was in rehab and immediately after. My discharge also required me to see a therapist and a psychiatrist. I continued to see both and eventually asked about getting back on stimulants again. I knew better, but I was miserable, and the psychiatrist said he saw no problem with it as long as I took it as prescribed. I did take it as prescribed this time. I also began to drink again. I wasn't drinking hard liquor now, I drank red wine, and I only drank at night, so I sort of felt better about that—but again, I knew better in my heart.

Our family owned a farm in the country about a half-hour from our home. It was completely isolated and a real "getaway." There is a two-bedroom home on the farm with a small spring-fed lake. I moved into the home with my dogs "temporarily," with the hope that it would be more peaceful there. It was more peaceful. There was nothing there but the home, and there were no other homes near it. I wanted to disappear, and I was able to almost disappear there—but the pain, the trauma, and my past did not disappear. They were following me.

I thought that if I got out to the farm and could find some peace and quiet, I could figure out how I could "get back on my feet again." I got out there, and I realized the pain had followed me, and I was hurting so deeply. I literally was dealing with anguish and torment in my mind and my body. I was drinking and taking pills again. I had lost everything I thought mattered, and I felt I had suffered great injustice. I was such a fighter at one time, but I had no more fight in me. I had no more hope. I lost all hope and entered into hopelessness. I saw no way out, and for the first time in my life, I had suicidal thoughts.

Then I began to plan it. I began to devise the plan of how I would do it and where I would do it. This plan did not bring me hope, but I thought it would bring me relief. I thought the pain would be over. I drank some wine, watched some television, and I went to bed. That night everything would change. I went to bed hopeless and suicidal, but I woke up the next morning full of hope and joy. This hope did not fade; in fact, it has never faded. The joy did not leave; in fact, I still have this joy. What happened to me over that night changed my destiny, my outlook, and my life forever.

You may also be wondering what happened after I left the capitol in Georgia. About two years later, that elected official was forced out of his position and stepped down and out of politics. An ethics complaint was eventually filed against him for having an "inappropriate" relationship with a lobbyist. Even though the complaint was later dismissed and he originally denied the affair, the affair became public. He would later step down from his leadership position in the wake of a public scandal.

Please pray with me.

Father, thank You for Your great mercy. Jesus, thank You for the cross. Your mercies are new every morning (Lamentations 3:23), and that mercy reaches into the darkest night. We pray for anyone who may be battling the spirit of suicide or death. Jesus, You defeated death, hell, and the grave. We rebuke every demonic spirit of death and suicide in the mighty name of Jesus and command these spirits to go! We speak to every spirit of depression, isolation, and loneliness, loose these people and let them go! We decree and declare freedom over everyone reading this prayer in the powerful and mighty name of Jesus. We pray for supernatural encounters that shift everything and change lives forever. We decree and declare resurrection life to flow and for new beginnings now. In Jesus' mighty name. Amen.

> "The eyes of the Lord are upon even the weakest worshipers who love him—those who wait in hope and expectation for the strong, steady love of God. God will deliver them from death, even the certain death of famine, with no one to help"
>
> (Psalm 33:18–19, TPT).

Chapter 6: A New Beginning

If you live in the city, you never really get to see the beauty of the stars at night. The city lights drown out the majesty of the night's sky and the splendor of the stars. That was just one of the things I began to appreciate about being out in the country. I was alone, and it was quiet, but at night the sky would speak volumes. I am reminded of what David wrote in Psalm 19:

> The heavens proclaim the glory of God. The skies display his craftsmanship. Day after day they continue to speak; night after night they make him known. They speak without a sound or word; their voice is never heard. Yet their message has gone throughout the earth, and their words to all the world...

Psalm 19:1–4 (NLT)

This night was different. I had quietly resolved that life was no longer worth living, and I was serious. I wanted out.

I climbed the stairs to the second-story loft and lay down in bed. I turned off the lights, and the room was totally dark, and I drifted off to sleep.

I'm not sure how long I had been asleep, but when I woke up, my room wasn't dark anymore. I was lying under the most beautifully bright night sky. This was not a dream. This was real, and I have to be honest, I was greatly alarmed by what I was experiencing. The room was electric. It was charged with something I had not ever experienced on that level before.

My natural mind began to search for what in the world could be happening because the roof of my home was gone, and I was literally lying under an open sky. My panic began to wane, and it gave

59

way to awe and wonder. I thought to myself, *This feels like heaven.*

I have only heard the audible voice of the Lord once in my life. That was in my fifth-grade classroom when the Lord called my name. What I experienced that night was the Lord speaking to my heart. We carried on an entire conversation without ever speaking a single word. No words were spoken. I knew His thoughts, and He heard mine.

I have heard many testimonies of people who have gone to heaven. Some have been there because of a near-death experience, and others have been taken to heaven. I am often reminded of my own experience in my bedroom when they speak of telepathic communication in heaven. Many testify of not speaking in heaven, but instead, thoughts are known without communicating with words. This was my experience in my bedroom.

Above my head was an open heaven, and all around me were portals. At the time, I described them or would have said they were "wormholes"; however, today, I would describe them as "portals." Where the walls of my bedroom were supposed to be, I was now looking into portals that were open and circular and constantly moving. There was no sound coming from these portals, and there had to be a dozen or more of them surrounding me in my bedroom. I remember the room being totally silent, but my heart was bursting with hope, and my life began to sing a new song. Looking back, I believe these portals were bringing another dimension into my room. It was the dimension of heaven.

Many examples of portals or "doorways" can be seen throughout Scripture.

"So wake up, you living gateways! Lift up your heads, you doorways of eternity! Welcome the King of Glory, for he is about to come through you" (Psalm 24:7, TPT).

"But he commanded the skies to open; he opened the doors of heaven" (Psalm 78:23 (NLT).

"Then he said, 'I tell you the truth, you will all see heaven open and the angels of God going up and down on the Son of Man, the one who is the stairway between heaven and earth'" (John 1:51, NLT).

"Then suddenly, after I wrote down these messages, I saw a portal open into the heavenly realm and the same trumpet-voice I heard speaking with me at the beginning said, 'Ascend into this realm! I want to reveal to you what must happen after this'" (Revelation 4:1, TPT).

What took place that night changed me forever. The Lord showered me with love, affection, encouragement, and much-needed direction. He literally showed me I was His daughter. I saw myself as a princess. What little girl doesn't dream of being a princess? Well, the God who created the heavens and the earth showed up in my bedroom to tell me that I was His very own daughter and because He was the King, that made me a princess.

I was ignorant at the time that Jesus was known as the "King of kings," but it all makes perfect sense to me today. Seeing myself as someone so loved and so cherished shifted my identity in a moment. I literally saw myself as His princess and His very own daughter. How did I see this? I actually saw what looked like a "movie" playing in my room. It was a divine reel of what the Lord wanted me to see. He played me a "movie," and it touched my heart in the most significant and deepest of ways possible. In a moment, He was erasing the pictures and the past that wanted to define and oppress me. He was showing me His plan and how He saw me through His eyes.

When I saw myself in this "movie," I was amazed. I was truly a sight to behold. I looked so beautiful and happy, and I gazed at myself in amazement. I was beyond amazed; I was astonished. I had never looked or felt more beautiful or more loved. This was such a contrast to who or what I had become accustomed to being. Prior to this experience, I had identified myself as a failure, an alcoholic, an addict, and I felt like I had a record playing in my mind with the question, "What is wrong with me?" Now I was sitting in my room with the Creator of the universe, and He was showing me something altogether different. I am reminded of the following scripture from Hosea:

> "But then I will win her back once again. I will lead her into the desert and speak tenderly to her there. I will return her vineyards to her and transform the Valley of Trouble into a gateway of hope. She will give herself to me there, as she did long ago when she was young, when I freed her from her captivity in Egypt. When that day comes," says the Lord, "you will call me 'my husband' instead of 'my master.' O Israel, I will wipe the many names of Baal from your lips, and you will never mention them again. On that day I will make a covenant with all the wild animals and birds of the sky and the animals that scurry along the ground so they will not harm you. I will remove all the weapons of war from the land, all swords and bows, so you can live unafraid in peace and safety. I will make you my wife forever, showing you righteousness and justice, unfailing love and compassion. I will be faithful to you and make you mine, and you will finally know me as the LORD."

> Hosea 2:14–20 (NLT)

On my wedding day, almost seven years later, I felt beautiful, loved, and celebrated. To this day, it is the only time that has even come remotely close to that night. He won my heart that night. I was His forever. Nothing and no one has ever proven to be more faithful than Him. He showed up in my absolute darkest moment and rescued me. I was totally isolated from anyone on a rural farm in the middle of nowhere. The devil thought he had won and had backed me into the final corner of suicide, but my Lord and my Savior showed up strong in my weakness (2 Corinthians 12:10).

I was shown so much that night, and to be honest, I did not understand it all. Later, as I read the Bible, the Lord would bring to my remembrance scenes and things from that night, and I could understand more of what I had been shown. One of the things I believe He showed me was that I was "His bride." Although I was unaware at the time of the Scriptures speaking of the "bride of Christ," I am now aware, and I believe that He was showing me that I am part of the bride of Christ. The bride of Christ is mentioned twice in the book of Revelation:

> Let us rejoice and exalt him and give him glory, because the wedding celebration of the Lamb has come. And his bride has made herself ready. Fine linen, shining bright and clear, has been given to her to wear, and the fine linen represents the righteous deeds of his holy believers. Then the angel said to me, "Write these words: Wonderfully blessed are those who are invited to feast at the wedding celebration of the Lamb!" And then he said to me, "These are the true words of God."

Revelation 19:7–9 (TPT)

I now believe that one of the reasons I looked so beautiful in this movie is because I was looking at myself in my own resurrected body and as part of the bride of Christ. I knew I was looking at me because it looked like me, but I looked quite close to perfection. I was distinctly more beautiful than I have even known or looked in my life. I was amazed, and I knew He wanted me to feel beautiful, and I knew He wanted me to feel His love. I felt so treasured, so celebrated, so cherished, and so adored. I knew He loved me, and I was in love with Him.

I'm not sure how long I sat in my room with the Lord under His starry sky because I totally lost all track of time. Time did not seem to matter or exist that night, and maybe that is because He operates outside of time. I sat with Him until I could not hold my eyes open any longer. I remember vividly thinking, *How could anyone be sleepy seeing and experiencing this?* I apologized to the Lord for being so tired, and I remember reluctantly but gently falling off to sleep. I woke up the next morning a new person and a new creation. The old me was dead, and the new me had been born again (2 Corinthians 5:17).

If you have never made Jesus Christ your personal Lord and Savior, I would like to invite you to make a decision that will transform your life and change your destiny in a moment. This prayer is simple, but it must be from the heart. The Lord looks on the heart, and this is important to understand.

"The Lord doesn't see things the way you see them. People judge by the outward appearance, but the Lord looks at the heart" (1 Samuel 16:7, NLT).

I believe the Lord saw the yes in my heart before I said yes to Him. On this night in my bedroom, I said yes in my heart, and I said yes to Him. If you have always had a yes in your heart, but you have never said yes to Him, I pray today is the day that the two become one.

Please pray with me.

Jesus, I love You. I need You. I want to begin a new life with You today. I'm ready to leave the past behind and start fresh. You make all things new (Revelation 21:5). I want to be new—I want to be born again. I believe You are the Son of God. I believe You were crucified, dead, and buried. I believe You rose again, and today You live—and You will live forever. Lord, please forgive my sin and wash me whiter than snow (Psalm 51:7). In Jesus' mighty name. Amen.

Chapter 7: The Road to Restoration

Over the next two months, the farm where I lived seemed to have come to new life, and I felt like a little child again. Immediately following my experience in my bedroom, I would continue to have these supernatural events at night and during the day. They were dramatic, powerful, and continued to be life-transforming. It was around this time that I started running again. Years earlier, I had loved running, and it became a part of my daily life at the farm. I would see signs and wonders in the sky as I ran.

The clouds would come together to form a cross, or I would literally see the form or face of Jesus in the sky and on the pavement as I would run. I felt Him on the dirt roads I ran, and I saw Him everywhere I went. It was an extraordinary time.

I was also still seeing the "movies" that would play for me in thin air. Later, I learned that these experiences are known as "visions," and there are many examples of them in Scripture. One such example is in Acts 10, where the Lord gave Peter a vision of a sheet falling from heaven along with an instruction.

"He saw the sky open, and something like a large sheet was let down by its four corners. In the sheet were all sorts of animals, reptiles, and birds. Then a voice said to him, 'Get up, Peter; kill and eat them'" (Acts 10:11–13, NLT).

The Apostle Paul received several visions recorded in Scripture that included ministry instructions and even warnings.

> That night Paul had a vision: A man from Macedonia in northern Greece was standing there, pleading with him, "Come over to Macedonia and help us!" So we decided

to leave for Macedonia at once, having concluded that
God was calling us to preach the Good News there.

Acts 16:9–10 (NLT)

"One night the Lord spoke to Paul in a vision and told him,
'Don't be afraid! Speak out! Don't be silent! For I am with you, and
no one will attack and harm you, for many people in this city belong
to me'" (Acts 18:9–10, NLT).

"After I returned to Jerusalem, I was praying in the Temple and
fell into a trance. I saw a vision of Jesus saying to me, 'Hurry! Leave
Jerusalem, for the people here won't accept your testimony about
me'" (Acts 22:17–18, NLT).

Again, because I did not know Scripture at the time, I was
ignorant. The Bible tells us in Hosea 4:6 that "My people perish for
lack of knowledge…" I was totally unaware that any of the things I
was witnessing were possible, and prior to this, I had most definitely
never heard of anyone having these experiences. My eyes had been
opened, and I kept wondering how I had gone all my life without
knowing Him and experiencing who He is. I was full of wonder
and awe. Life suddenly had so much meaning, and I felt so tenderly
loved and fiercely watched over. I know the farm wasn't Eden, but
for a season, it certainly felt close. And as the garden of Eden was a
beginning, so also was the farm a new beginning for me.

I spent that fall falling in love again. I had found my first love, and
this time when He called my name, I answered, "Here I am Lord, send
me" (Isaiah 6:8). The honeymoon had begun, and it was an unforgettable
and remarkable time. Words fail me and fall short in describing the
magnificence of it all. The Lord displayed His glory for me in new and
creative ways almost every day, and I continued to be awed and amazed.

I am particularly reminded of a night during that time that will forever be etched in my heart and mind. I felt I was supposed to drive down to another part of the farm where there were acres of open fields. I drove down about dusk and walked the property until there was little light left to see. No one lived on this property at the time, and there was no one on the property but me when this took place. What happened that night was like the grand finale at a fireworks show, but there were no fireworks and no sound. It was completely silent, with the exception of my iPod that was playing music to what I would call the grandest display of splendor I have ever witnessed.

It was similar to what took place in my bedroom weeks earlier, but it took place on a much larger and grander scale. First, it spanned an area that was larger than a football field. This time the night sky was just a backdrop for what would unfold. The closest thing I could describe it to was a "laser light show," but that doesn't do it justice. Again, it's really hard to put into words seeing a heavenly light show that displayed the supernatural on such a grand scale. It was breathtaking, magnificent, and glorious. It lasted for what had to be a few hours. Again, I lost all track of time. Heaven had invaded earth, and I was right in the middle of it. I never wanted it to end. When it was over, I walked back to my car and headed to the cabin. I was amazed and undone by all I had witnessed.

As December approached, I made plans to drive back to Atlanta for a quick trip. This would be one of the worst decisions I made during that time. I should have stayed put and enjoyed the open heaven I was living under, but I lacked the wisdom and understanding at the time to discern the matter. I was being led back to the battlefield by the enemy, and I did not know it.

In December, I drove back to Atlanta and checked into my hotel in the heart of Buckhead. I looked out over the city and took in the panoramic view. My room was located on a higher floor, and I had an unobstructed view of the city all around me. I did some shopping at the mall right across from my hotel, and when I made it back to my room, it was already dark. I looked out over the city, and suddenly, I realized my spiritual eyes had been opened. I was seeing the unseen spiritual world that operated in Atlanta, in addition to the natural world that we all can see.

In 2 Kings 6, Elisha prays for his servant's eyes to be opened during the battle at Dothan. His servant was terrified when he saw that they were indeed surrounded by their enemies, but Elisha instructed him to not be afraid and prayed for his eyes to be opened:

> "Don't be afraid!" Elisha told him. "For there are more on our side than on theirs!" Then Elisha prayed, "O LORD, open his eyes and let him see!" The LORD opened the young man's eyes, and when he looked up, he saw that the hillside around Elisha was filled with horses and chariots of fire.
>
> 2 Kings 6:16–17 (NLT)

The hillside was filled with the Lord's army, but they were not visible to the natural eye. Elisha could see them, but he had to pray for his servant to see, and he did.

> As the Aramean army advanced toward him, Elisha prayed, "O LORD, please make them blind." So the Lord struck them with blindness as Elisha had asked. Then Elisha went out and told them, "You have come the

wrong way! This isn't the right city! Follow me and I will take you to the man you are looking for."

2 Kings 6:18–19 (NLT)

It didn't take me long to realize that I had also "come the wrong way" and was not in the right city. I stood at the window and could not believe what I was seeing with my own two eyes. It's no wonder I was having such a hard time in Atlanta. I was seeing some of the warfare and principalities waring over the city, but again I did not understand so much of what I was seeing because I did not know the Word of God.

In Ephesians 6, the Apostle Paul describes the word of God as being like a sword. In fact, he calls it the sword of the Spirit. He also warns Christians to put on the full armor of God for battle every day.

A final word: Be strong in the Lord and in his mighty power. Put on all of God's armor so that you will be able to stand firm against all strategies of the devil. For we are not fighting against flesh-and-blood enemies, but against evil rulers and authorities of the unseen world, against mighty powers in this dark world, against evil spirits in the heavenly places. Therefore, put on every piece of God's armor so you will be able to resist the enemy in the time of evil. Then after the battle you will still be standing firm.

Ephesians 6:10–13 (NLT)

I was seeing the mighty powers at work in the world and the evil spirits in the heavenly places. I also saw what looked like giants, or they could have been large angels, walking on the sidewalk below.

I could see people who were normal in size and stature, and then there would be what looked like a giant human that was significantly larger in the crowds below. These larger beings were scattered among the people below. It was around this time that I began to realize I was becoming quite fearful. Through the night, I experienced some terrifying visions and began to fear for my life.

I felt the Lord tell me to not eat. So I did not eat. I also did not drink anything. I was unaware of the spiritual discipline of fasting at the time, but unbeknownst to me, I had started my first full fast, and it lasted for three days. During that time, the battle was fierce, and then suddenly, after three days, a scripture entered into my mind and came alive in my heart. I knew I had heard it when I was a child. It is now one of my most favorite scriptures and near and dear to my heart like none other.

"...with God all things are possible" (Matthew 19:26, NKJV).

During the three days of fasting, I had seen an open vision of my car flipping and being destroyed. The message was clear to me at the time: "If you get in your car, you will die on the road home." I had seen this vision, but it was not from God. This was one of the many lessons I learned the hard way. The Bible tells us to test the spirits to see if they are from God (1 John 4:1).

We must know the Word of God and test our revelation, vision, or dreams with the Word of God. If you do not know the Word of God, you have lost the battle before it has even begun. There is grace and mercy for every new believer and baby Christian, but at some point, you will have to learn the Word of God and let it transform your heart and mind to walk out a victorious Christian life.

Somewhere during my life, the short phrase *"...with God all things are possible"* had made its way into my heart. I don't know when or where, but when I needed it, I found it in my heart. I concluded that if *"all things are possible,"* then God could keep my car from crashing, and I wouldn't die. I know this may sound ridiculous, but I saw with my own two eyes my car flip and crash into pieces with me in it. That was scary, and it intimidated me greatly. I also saw many other things during those three days that were intimidating, but with the Word of God in my heart and faith that He would get me home safely, I packed my bags and drove south.

It was obvious on the four-hour drive back to the farm that the warfare I had encountered in Atlanta was following me, although not anywhere near the magnitude or scale that I had encountered in Atlanta. My spiritual eyes were also still open, so I was actually able to see the warfare clearly. It was dark when I drove down the drive to the cabin. As I brought in my bags, I stopped on the deck to take in what was happening in the sky all around the home. Half of the sky was lit up with green light to the right of me, and to the left of me, the entire sky was lit up with red light. I could clearly see that the two sides were warring, and I knew the battle was over me. Now I believe that the battle I was seeing in the spirit was over my destiny.

In Revelation 4, John, the beloved apostle, describes the Lord's throne and mentions that it was surrounded by green light:

> Instantly I was taken into the spirit realm, and behold—I saw a heavenly throne being set in place and someone seated upon it. His appearance was sparkling like crystal and glowing like a carnelian gemstone. Surrounding the throne was a circle of green light, like an emerald rainbow.

> Revelation 4:2–3 (TPT)

I was keenly aware that I was watching a battle of good versus evil. I watched this from my front deck on the cabin for some time before I went inside. I walked to the table in the center of the cabin and began to speak to the Lord out loud about all that was taking place. I didn't understand all that was happening, and to be honest, I just wanted to go to bed. I felt like I had just escaped the battle of my life, and now it looked like that battle had followed me home. The Lord was speaking to my heart, and it gave me peace. I was speaking with Him, and I knew everything was going to be okay.

Then, I saw something that my eyes could hardly believe. I saw something materialize out of thin air and fall on the table in front of me. It was a diamond. I heard it hit the table, and it bounced a few times before it stopped and lay perfectly still in front of me. It was cut perfectly and sparkling with perfection. I did not even know what to do with it. To be honest, I was scared to touch it. I got up as close as possible and looked and looked. At the time, I was wearing my great-grandmother's diamond ring that was over two carats. This diamond looked to be larger, and I believed it to be a gift from God to me.

It was at that exact moment that I could see car lights coming up the drive. *No*, I thought. *I want to see this diamond.*

The car lights kept coming, and this was extremely abnormal for the farm and especially at this time of night. I walked outside and saw it was two patrol cars. The officers informed me that they had papers to take me back to Atlanta to the same treatment facility where I had previously been months earlier. I didn't know what "papers" they had, but I felt quite sure they were either not legal or based on misinformation. This time I would not go quietly.

I protested loudly. I also had the Lord with me, so this time was going to be different. I had Him with me the first time I was taken away, but I did not know Him, although He knew me. This time I knew Him, and we were on this journey together. I began to argue and dispute the situation, but in the end, I had no choice. Reluctantly,

I was forced into the back of the patrol car. The last place in the world I wanted to go back to was Atlanta, but against my will, I was driven back down the same road I had just traveled.

With everything I had been through and seen with the Lord, I knew He could do anything. I began to pray out loud, "With God, all things are possible. With God, all things are possible. With God, all things are possible..." I repeated this prayer and repeated it again and again. I'm not sure what I was expecting Him to do, but I truly believed He could miraculously get me out of that patrol car and save me from being taken back to the battlefront in Atlanta.

While He did not save me from being taken back to Atlanta and the rehabilitation hospital, He was with me through it all. This time I would experience His peace and even His joy in the midst of the trial. He spoke very clearly to me and gave me very specific instructions on how to deal with the doctors and the situations I would face in the hospital.

In the early morning hours, I was checked into the hospital. The doctors then proceeded to prescribe new medications for me to take, but the Lord told me to refuse them all. I did. I never took any new medications while I was there, and I refused treatment.

This all happened a few days before Christmas in 2007. I stayed in this hospital for two weeks and over Christmas, and though I was angry and at times distraught over the situation, I decided to make the best of it. The Lord comforted me and showered me with His love and peace. On Christmas day, when everyone had family and visitors, I sat alone with an empty chair next to me. In the natural, this could have been a real moment to feel deeply saddened and alone, but it was one of the best moments I can remember during that time. I felt the Lord come and sit next to me. I felt His peace, and I felt His love flood me. I remember smiling and sitting back, enjoying His presence. He was my family now, and He was with me. I was learning for myself the powerful truth that if God is for you, who can dare be against you? (Hebrews 13:6)

I was released after two weeks. Since I rode in a patrol car there, I needed to get back to the farm somehow. I bought a one-way ticket to the closest airport to the farm and saw the Lord provide miraculously along the way. A cab dropped me off at the gate of the farm with my suitcase, and I walked down the long road to the cabin where I had just been two weeks earlier.

It was midday, and it was a new year. The farm was quiet then, and you would have never known any of the events that had taken place there had ever even happened. I opened the door of the cabin and went straight to the table to find my diamond. I may have been taken on a detour, but now I found myself exactly in the place where I had left off.

The diamond was gone. I looked on the floor and crawled around on my hands and knees. No diamond. I was deeply saddened and discouraged. I felt like something really precious had been stolen from me, and in truth, it had. Then I realized that the Lord had created that diamond, and if He wanted to do it again, He could. I spent the next few days resting because the battle had been fierce, but I was beginning to learn that the battle belongs to the Lord (2 Chronicles 20:15).

Please pray with me.

Father, we thank You that You will never leave us nor forsake us (Hebrews 13:5). Thank You for showing us such great mercy and love. We pray for Your comfort to comfort those facing persecution of any kind. We decree and declare that righteousness and justice are the foundation of Your throne, and mercy and truth go before You (Psalm 89:14). Lord, we pray for those who have faced great injustice and have suffered. We pray for Your justice and mercy to flood them and their circumstances. We speak and believe that Your perfect will is coming to pass in their lives right now and that you are working all things together for their good (Romans 8:28). We pray all this in the powerful and mighty name of Jesus Christ! Amen.

Chapter 8: New Horizons

It was early January 2008 as I awoke from a very vivid dream. I sat up in bed and looked around. The dramatic events of the last few weeks were always in my thoughts. Even after I had arrived back at the farm, I feared that it would not be long until the same authorities—or someone else—would show up and would try to do something similar—or even worse. The traumatic experiences I had been through felt like they were always replaying in my mind. I was also fighting a great deal of anger and bitterness over the events, and I was unaware of the significance of the biblical principle of "forgiveness." All the unforgiveness, bitterness, and offense I was harboring were creating a great deal of pain in my life. I believe this also opened the door for more attacks and deception.

I had only been back at the farm a few days when I dreamed a dream that would become a reality. I dreamed of flying back to the Caribbean but the dream felt more like an instruction to move there. I did not know how to pray—and I did not have a foundation of biblical truth or wisdom to stand on—but I did have a dream. I had learned to be attentive to my dreams and began to realize that many things I saw and experienced were coming to pass in my daily life. I also felt an urgency in the dream to go quickly.

> For God speaks again and again, though people do not recognize it. He speaks in dreams, in visions of the night, when deep sleep falls on people as they lie in their beds. He whispers in their ears and terrifies them with warnings. He makes them turn from doing wrong; He keeps them from pride. He protects them from the grave, from crossing over the river of death.

Job 33:14–18 (NLT)

I made the necessary preparations to travel. I thought I was going to find a place to live and that I would be back in a few days to get everything together, but when I got to the island, I felt the Lord tell me not to go back. I had only brought a few items to wear and everything I had with me fit in a small suitcase. This was a new development, but I trusted Him. He had not failed me yet, and I truly believed He would not fail me now.

I stayed in hotels while I searched for a home, and I found the perfect place overlooking the Atlantic ocean. It was a one-bedroom guest home that was part of a larger property that had just been built. No one had ever even lived there before me. It was stunning, and the view was spectacular. From my home, the view out over the Atlantic was as far as the eye could see. I moved in quickly and enjoyed the privacy I had. It was a secluded location, and it felt like a million miles from the drama I had just been through. At that moment, I wanted to live there forever. No one but the Lord and me knew exactly where I was living, and that was how I wanted it.

During that time, the Lord began to teach me how to journal my dreams, and I began to learn a little about dream interpretation. I also began to rent and watch videos about the Bible. I am a visual learner, so seeing the Bible stories as movies was a good place for me to begin to learn the basics. I would often watch the movies over and over again. I also found a small church to attend. The Lord provided all I needed, and I never went without anything.

During this time, a lot of healing took place, and it was very helpful to be somewhere for an extended period of time without great fear. I would still need much healing in my heart and soul, but that would be an ongoing process. At the time, it was good to just be still and know He is God; He is good, and He is faithful. I was learning to trust again. I was learning to discern His voice, and I had come to learn the hard way that not every voice or every spirit was holy or the Lord. Paul addresses this in 2 Corinthians 11:14 (NLT) when he states that, "Even Satan disguises himself as an angel of light."

I found this to be true, but the Lord is faithful. Even when I lacked the wisdom and understanding to discern His voice, the Lord would flood my situation with His grace and mercy. I spent four and half months on the island until I had a dream that showed me it was time to go back to the farm. To be honest, I did not want to go at first. I was quick to jump on the plane to the Caribbean, but I spoke with the Lord a lot about leaving. "Speaking with the Lord" was how I prayed then. I did not know how to pray, but I would talk with Him, and He would speak back to me. Now I know that is praying. I was praying all the time because I was speaking to Him all the time, and He was always speaking with me. I am also reminded of what the Apostle Paul said in 1 Thessalonians 5:17 (NLT) when he tells us to "Never stop praying."

I did eventually leave the island and return to the US. I moved back to the farm and enjoyed the quiet farm life without any more interruptions for about the next two years. Beazy and Bogey were back with me again, and that made me very happy. I also began to study the Scriptures, watch hours of Christian television daily, become active in my local church, and I eventually began working at the same ministry where I had once done my community service. My life was being transformed. And while I had been redeemed in a moment, I was now being restored. It was a special time that I will always remember with fondness and great affection.

Please pray with me.

Father, thank You that You meet us where we are. You do not require us to be perfect to come to You. In fact, if we were perfect, we would not need You—but we are not perfect—and we do need You. You are the only perfect One, Jesus. We honor You, and we love You. Thank You, Jesus, for the cross. Thank You for making a way for us to be one with You. You live in us, and we are in You, and we are one with You. We pray for more of You, Jesus. Please help us to be teachable and to learn Your ways. Your ways are not our ways (Isaiah 55:8). Help us become like little children (Matthew 18:3) with childlike faith and to lean not to our own understanding (Proverbs 3:5). Teach us to number our days that we may gain a heart of wisdom (Psalm 90:12). Father, some of us have faced situations that have wounded us deeply. We pray for healing and wholeness in our souls, and we ask that You would help us to forgive those who have wronged us. We choose to forgive them with all our hearts, and we release them. They owe us nothing. Lord, we trust You and leave it all to Your righteous justice (Romans 12:19). We also pray against the spirit of trauma. Father, only You can heal a shattered soul. We take authority over trauma and the traumatic memories that would haunt Your children. We thank You for removing these memories and replacing them with new creation memories rooted and grounded in You, Lord. Thank You for healing the brokenhearted and bandaging their wounds (Psalm 147:3). In Jesus' mighty name. Amen.

Chapter 9: A Heart's Desire

Living on a farm by yourself in the rural south wasn't normal—at least not for a single girl my age. I came to realize at this point that my life was no longer "normal" and that it would never be "normal." I was okay with that part. I had Him, and He was all I needed. I had more peace and joy in my life at the farm than I had ever experienced previously. I was learning how priceless peace truly is, and I could not believe I had spent so much of my life without it. My "normal" life before Jesus had no peace, and to compensate for this, I drank alcohol, took prescription pills, shopped, indulged in empty relationships, and countless other counterfeits to fill the void of where the Lord should have been in life. These counterfeits did provide some temporary entertainment or fun, but they did not satisfy and only left me feeling emptier.

At the farm—even though I was alone—I was not alone, and I had more peace and joy than I had ever known. He was with me, and He was all I needed. Still, I was in my early thirties, and I had always dreamed of being a wife and mother. After my conversion, this desire became even stronger. I was also clean and sober now. The only pills I took were multivitamins. My life looked totally different, and I began to dream of sharing it with someone who loved the Lord like me. It quickly became my heart's desire.

"Take delight in the Lord, and He will give you your heart's desires" (Psalm 37:4, NLT).

I began reading and studying the Word every day. I had purchased a new Bible and a plan to read it cover to cover in one year. I did it in a few weeks. When I read the Bible all the way through the first time, I just started over again. I was watching hours of Christian preaching and teaching daily. I was so hungry for God, and I just wanted to know more and learn more. I found it endlessly fascinating. And although it was a process—and it did not happen overnight—I eventually gave up all secular music. I began to incorporate some Christian music into my listening and gradually added more. In time, I found I had no desire to listen to secular music anymore. To this day, all the music I grew up listening to is just something from the past. Most of it sounds and feels so empty when I do hear it at the grocery store or shopping—and that's because without God in it, it is empty to me.

I began attending one of the largest denominational churches in our area, and they had a vibrant "Celebrate Recovery" program. Celebrate Recovery is a Christ-centered addiction recovery program. I loved being with other Christians and being honest and vulnerable about addiction. I loved going to church and tried to be there every time the doors opened. I enjoyed having a Christian community around me and being a part of a growing church. I got baptized and felt like anything was possible again. My life was totally different from anything I could have ever imagined just a few years earlier, but it was the best life I had ever lived, and I was truly happy.

The pastor of our church and his wife wanted to introduce me to another pastor in their denomination who was single. They had invited him to come to preach at our church and wanted me to go to dinner with them while he was in town. I was more than excited and agreed without reservation. When I heard this pastor preach at our church from the book of Revelation and saw the passion in him, I was beyond encouraged. I was overjoyed—it was almost euphoric.

A small group of us went to dinner together that night. It was my pastor and his wife, another couple, and the visiting pastor and myself. He was tall and handsome, and he obviously loved the Lord. The dinner was wonderful, and I was starting to wonder if all my dreams were about to come true. When it was time to leave, he asked me if it would be okay for him to email me. I quickly said, "Yes," and gave him my email. I walked out of the home on cloud nine and got into my car. As I drove home to the farm, I heard the still small voice of the Lord whisper to my heart, "Fast."

Fasting had become a part of my journey with the Lord. I obviously had learned from my experience in Atlanta how powerful fasting could be. I felt the Lord had asked me early in my walk to fast one day a week. I had been living a lifestyle of fasting one day a week for many months, but when I heard Him speak to me about fasting on my drive home, I knew this was different. I began to pray as I drove and knew He was asking me to fast longer than just a day. I felt He was asking me to fast about the situation with the pastor I had just met, and I wanted to hear from heaven on this. As exciting as it was, I knew from many past experiences how devastating the wrong person at the wrong time could be. I wanted to know from the Lord if this was the man He intended to be my husband—and if it wasn't, I didn't want a thing to do with it.

I fasted for the next seven days. It was a total fast, and I only drank water and had some chicken broth a few nights. It was not easy, but I felt the Lord in every minute of that fast. I was drawing near to Him, and He was drawing near to me (James 4:8). I prayed from my heart that only the Lord's will be done in my life, and I wanted that to include who I dated and married. I knew in my heart He had someone special set apart for me, and I only wanted His best for my life and my husband. On the seventh day—it was a Sunday—I felt the Lord lead me to a tiny church that I had never been to before, but I knew a lady who went there. I was the only white person in the congregation that day, and I was happy in the Lord to be exactly where I was in that moment. That was one of the best church services

I had even been a part of up until that time. I left full of the joy of the Lord.

On the ride home to the farm, I spoke with the Lord. I told Him I really would like to eat and that I was hungry. I also asked Him if the young preacher was my husband. I heard back as clear as could be—not audibly—but clearly, I heard in my heart, "Seek first My Kingdom and all these things shall be added to you" (Matthew 6:33). I knew that was in the Bible, but I did not know where. I rushed home and found the entire scripture to study.

"Seek the Kingdom of God above all else, and live righteously, and he will give you everything you need" (Matthew 6:33, NLT).

It was clear the Lord was telling me not to "seek a husband" but instead to seek Him. I knew that my husband would come as a result of my relationship with the Lord. I also felt released to break my fast. That night, I got an email from the young preacher. It was nice, but it was short, and the message was clear. He told me it was nice to meet me, and he wished me well in my walk with the Lord. It was a courteous "goodbye" email. I knew He had been praying too, and it was well with my soul. I was trusting the Lord for His best, and I knew it would happen in His time.

Shortly after this, I was exercising at the farm and listening to Christian music. I felt the Lord speak something to my heart so clearly. He said, "If you will wait and not date, I will bring your mate straight to you." Yes, it rhymes, so it's easy to remember. This very statement I would restate to myself over and over during the years of waiting that would follow. The Lord was asking me to trust Him to bring me my husband. I knew He was asking me to not date in the meantime. He wanted me to totally trust Him on this, and I said, "Yes, Lord." I thought it would be something that would happen soon, but it would take many years of waiting without dating for this to come to pass.

Looking back, I didn't need to be dating, and I didn't need to be married at that time. The Lord needed to do deep work in my life to prepare me for marriage and to heal my heart and deliver me from hurts from my past. I'm so grateful that He is so faithful and such a good, good Father. He knows exactly what we need and when we need it. We can trust Him, but early in my walk, I was still learning the very basics of trusting. Being in my early thirties, then mid-thirties, and then transitioning into my late thirties and not dating was challenging. At times I would face waves of fear and unbelief that told me I was just wasting my time and that I would be too old to marry and have children if I waited any longer. These were all lies, but in the final few months, right before I met the man who would become my husband, it became increasingly difficult, and I really had to fight to stay in faith.

The Lord gave me prophetic words and dreams that helped me greatly and encouraged me. A few years before I met my husband, I saw him in a dream. In the dream, I was looking at a couple— from behind—holding hands in front of snow-covered mountains. Because I was looking from behind, I could not see their faces, but I could see details about each of them. In the dream, I knew the girl was me, and the man I was holding hands with was my husband in the future. He was tall, slim, and had a full head of dark hair. I wasn't sure what the mountains meant, but at the time, I figured it symbolized the mountains we would face together in the Lord.

This dream not only encouraged me—it helped me stay on track. Many times people would try to do their own matchmaking, and while I believe their intentions were good, it was not helpful. They would show me a photo or point out a person to me. When I would see that they were balding or maybe have blonde hair or something similar, I would tell them, "That's not my husband." They would usually respond perplexed, "Well, how do you know?" I would quickly tell them that I had already seen my husband in a dream and he didn't look like that.

I would meet my husband in Colorado Springs, Colorado, many years later. The mountains in my dream were the Front Range section of the Southern Rocky Mountains that run through Colorado Springs. When I stepped off the plane the first time flying into Colorado, I knew those were the mountains in my dream with my husband. It was on my first trip to Colorado that I met my husband. I knew in my heart the first time I saw him that he was the one. I wasn't 100 percent sure, but I was fairly certain. We would be married a little over a year later.

But the years of waiting before I met my husband were so important in my walk with the Lord. I waited over six years and they were intimate, wonderful, and challenging years, and I needed every minute of that time to prepare for the many demands of marriage and, eventually, children. I surrendered my life to Christ at thirty-two, and I was married at thirty-eight. Our first son was born ten days after I turned forty, and I was forty-two when our second son was born.

The Lord fulfilled His word to me, "If you will wait and not date, I will bring your mate straight to you." He did it just as He had said. Maybe it didn't happen when I wanted it to happen—but it did happen. Trusting His timing and His way is truly the best way. This is part of surrendering, and it is also a process. Truly I understand Proverbs 13:12 (NLT), "Hope deferred makes the heart sick, but a dream fulfilled is a tree of life."

Please pray with me.

Lord, thank You for being such a good, good Father (2 Corinthians 6:18). You know exactly what we need and when we need it (Matthew 6:8). You go before us to make our paths straight, and You are always with us (Deuteronomy 31:8). We are never alone, and You will never forsake us (Hebrews 13:5). You've instructed us to find our delight in You, and You will give us our heart's desire (Psalm 37:4). Please help us to do that—to find our delight in You first and know that everything else flows and follows from there. Help us to seek first Your Kingdom and to live righteously, and we will trust You to give us everything we need (Matthew 6:33). Help us to truly trust You and surrender to Your process and Your ways. We know Your ways are not our ways, Lord (Isaiah 55:8). Help us to learn and follow Your ways. We decree and declare, "Grace, grace to every mountain we face" (Zechariah 4:7). In Jesus' mighty name. Amen.

Chapter 10: Revival Fire

I moved to the farm in the summer of 2007, and while I was gone for several months to the Carribean, I did not fully move out and leave the farm until the summer of 2010. I always found it encouraging to know that the Apostle Paul spent about three years alone after his conversion in what many refer to as his "desert years."

> But then God called me by his grace, and chose me from my birth to be his. He was pleased to unveil his Son in me so that I would proclaim him to the peoples of the world. After I had this encounter, I kept it a secret for some time, sharing it with no one. And I had no desire to run to Jerusalem and try to impress those who had become apostles before me. Instead, I withdrew into the Arabian Desert. Then I returned to Damascus, where I had first encountered Jesus. I remained there for three years until I eventually went up to Jerusalem, met the apostle Peter, and stayed with him for a couple of weeks. The only other apostle I met during that time was Jacob, the Lord's brother.
>
> Galatians 1:15–19 (TPT)

My years at the farm were wonderful and, at times, very challenging. I occasionally fought fears about being alone so far from others. I had no firearms or any sort of weapon, but the Lord gave me real peace about this and told me His angels were more than able to take care of me (Psalm 91:11). He wanted me to trust Him and believe Him.

I had begun praying with a group of ladies who were all part of a local ministry in my hometown. This was the same ministry where I had done my community service before my conversion. The ministry had a job opening, and it needed to be filled, and we were praying as a group for the Lord to bring someone to fill the position. I needed a job, and within a few days, I had one. I was hired as a van driver to pick up children after school and carry them to the ministry, where they would spend their afternoons. I was overjoyed to be working with precious children and to be working for a ministry. I loved it, and I fell in love with the kids.

Since I did not have children of my own, I found myself loving these kids like my own. The pay wasn't much, and compared to some of the things I had done in my past, it may not have looked as exciting from the outside—but I was happy, and my heart was so full. I felt like my life had real purpose and that I was actually making a difference in the lives of others.

I am reminded of an experience I had after I had just started working at this ministry. I was an assistant teacher when I wasn't driving the van. The kids would spend time in class learning Bible stories and scriptures, and I would help where needed. Since I was helping with the five-year-old boys, this meant I would be taking the little boys to the restroom. I would wait for them in the hall and from there make sure they were behaving while in the bathroom. I think I was just having a bad day, but I remember vividly waiting outside the bathroom and speaking to the Lord. "Lord," I said. "I have a degree in journalism, and here I am waiting for little boys using the bathroom!" This wasn't my normal mindset, and it was most likely just the result of a bad day, but I heard back clearly in my heart His voice and His word. He said, "If you are faithful in little, I will make you faithful in much" (Luke 16:10).

In Luke 16:10 (TPT), the scripture states that "The one who faithfully manages the little he has been given will be promoted and trusted with greater responsibilities. But those who cheat with the little they have been given will not be considered trustworthy to receive more." The Lord wasn't saying these little children were insignificant. Quite the contrary. I discovered His great love for them every day, and I was amazed by it. He was telling me that the task of "bathroom breaks" may seem small, but if I was faithful in the small things, He would trust me with greater responsibilities. I felt Him so deeply in that moment, and I knew it to be the truth. I resolved to trust the Lord and do every task "unto Him" with all my heart. As Colossians 3:23 (TPT) states, "Put your heart and soul into every activity you do, as though you are doing it for the Lord himself and not merely for others."

Soon the teacher I was assisting left the ministry, and I was promoted to her position. I was now teaching a classroom of five-year-old boys, and it was a demanding job, but it was the most rewarding one I had ever had up until that moment. I loved "my boys" and prayed over them day and night to become "mighty men of valor" in the Lord. I felt the Lord had very special assignments and destinies for each one of them. They were a special group, and it was a special time.

It was around this time that I began traveling to a revival in Mobile, Alabama. I began going almost every weekend and was touched with the fire of God. I was experiencing things I did not even know were possible. I was clueless that these things even took place in church. My eyes had been opened to another world, and I had found a new addiction—revival!

What I experienced in these revival services touched and changed my life. The services were full of the heavy, weighty glory and presence of God. I did not even know what that was until I first experienced revival during those wonderful months in the fall of 2010. I would go to those services and encounter revival, see miracles, signs, and wonders, and then I would carry the revival back to my job at the ministry and pour it into the kids I worked with and loved. The results were amazing, and I began to see real fruit.

A young girl, almost totally deaf, began to hear again. The boys in my class were creating drawings of Jesus returning and vibrant pictures of God's fire and Holy Spirit. Several of my five-year-old boys were baptized in the Holy Spirit and began speaking in tongues. I saw turnarounds and miracles in children who were often defiant and difficult and watched them transform into being happy, peaceful, and well-behaved. I was changing too. It was obvious to me, and it was clear to others. I learned quickly that not everyone is going to love you being "set on fire." A boldness comes with that fire that can be offensive to others.

We can see this in Acts 2:

> On the day Pentecost was being fulfilled, all the disciples were gathered in one place. Suddenly they heard the sound of a violent blast of wind rushing into the house from out of the heavenly realm. The roar of the wind was so overpowering it was all anyone could bear! Then all at once a pillar of fire appeared before their eyes. It separated into tongues of fire that engulfed each one of them. They were all filled and equipped with the Holy Spirit and were inspired to speak in tongues—empowered by the Spirit to speak in languages they had never learned!
>
> Acts 2:1–4 (TPT)

Further in Acts 2, it says that the people of the city were drawn to this home and to what was unfolding there because of the roaring sound. Apparently, they had created quite a scene. It goes on to say in verses 12–13 that some of the onlookers were astonished and dumbfounded, while others mocked and thought the disciples were just drunk.

I now understand, in part, how these onlookers could have thought the disciples were drunk. What I experienced in revival felt much like a very pure and unadulterated form of intoxication. Make no mistake, it was holy and beautiful, but it was also exhilarating, thrilling, and euphoric.

On my very first night in revival, I saw the lead evangelist lay hands on a man standing right next to me. This man was inches from me when what looked like a bolt of electricity began to hit him and threw him to the floor. On the floor, he began to shake and vibrate with great force—almost violently—and this went on for quite some time. I had a front-row seat to something I had never witnessed before, and I was amazed and awed. This was powerful, and there was no doubt about it; it was real. I wanted to experience what this man next to me had experienced, but when the evangelist prayed for me, nothing happened.

To be honest, I left the first night very disappointed that I had not experienced more of what I was seeing unfold around me, and I inquired of the Lord when I got back to my hotel room. The Lord reminded me of a broadcast I had seen on a Christian television network where people were falling on the ground, very similar to what I had just witnessed in the revival service that night. When I had seen the broadcast, I had wondered, *What are they doing?* To be honest, it offended me at the time. I was born again, but I had never experienced that nor seen it for myself. I concluded it must be fake or that people were just performing. I also remember speaking against it in the moment and complaining to the Lord about it. I believe my words and judgments were a block to me being able to receive what the Lord wanted to do for me in revival. He reminded me of all this. I spoke against it in ignorance, but now that I had seen it with my own eyes, I had no doubt that I had judged wrongly. I sincerely repented from my heart for speaking against it in ignorance and prayed that the Lord would touch me powerfully.

The next night I went back, and when I was prayed for, I was "slain in the Spirit." Some people also call this experience "falling under the power." Both these terms are used in Pentecostal and Charismatic Christian circles to describe the experience of falling to the floor under the power of the Holy Spirit. There are scriptural precedents for this throughout the Bible.

"...At that moment a thick cloud filled the Temple of the LORD. The priests could not continue their service because of the cloud, for the glorious presence of the LORD filled the Temple of God" (2 Chronicles 5:13–14, NLT).

"When I saw him, I fell at his feet as if I were dead. But he laid his right hand on me and said, 'Don't be afraid! I am the First and the Last. I am the living one. I died, but look—I am alive forever and ever! And I hold the keys of death and the grave'" (Revelation 1:17–18, NLT).

"So he [Paul] obtained the authorization and left for Damascus. Just outside the city, a brilliant light flashing from heaven and suddenly exploded all around him. Falling to the ground, he heard a booming voice say to him, 'Saul, Saul, why are you persecuting me?'" (Acts 9:3–4, TPT)

My first experience of "falling under the power" was exciting and euphoric. A minister came and laid his hand on my head, and my body instantly went limp as I fell gently to the floor. A man who was behind me caught me as I fell. As I lay on the floor, I felt a flood of peace, joy, and elation. It was as if time was almost standing still, and I was quietly alone with the Lord somewhere special. I could still hear all the people around me and the worship music playing, but in that moment, they were all being drowned out by Him. I felt like the Lord was personally ministering to me, and in fact, He was, through the Holy Spirit. I'm not sure how long I lay on the floor that night with Him, but when I got up, I felt different. I was still me, but I was different.

When I would travel to Mobile to go to these revival services, I would leave early on Friday afternoon so that I could get to the evening service. It was about a three-hour drive from my hometown. There was always a Friday and Saturday evening service, and then there was a Sunday morning church service. The spiritual warfare over going to Mobile was so intense that I had learned it was best for me to fast. I would begin fasting before I would leave Friday morning, and I would not break my fast until I left Mobile Sunday afternoon. I attended these revival services from early fall 2010 through the spring of 2011.

As I was being filled with the fire of the Holy Spirit, I was being totally transformed. After months of going to these meetings, I was learning to flow in the river of revival. Where at first I was gently falling to the ground under the power, I eventually began to find myself having more "explosive" encounters. It's no surprise as John the Baptist spoke of this in Luke 3. But John made it clear by telling them, "There is one coming who is mightier than I. He is supreme. In fact, I'm not worthy of even being his slave. I can only baptize you in this river, but he will baptize you into the Spirit of holiness and into his raging fire" (Luke 3:16, TPT).

You can also see this in Acts 1, "But I promise you this—the Holy Spirit will come upon you, and you will be seized with power. You will be my messengers to Jerusalem, throughout Judea, the distant provinces—even to the remotest places on earth!" (Acts 1:8, TPT)

The word "power" in the original Greek is actually the word *dunamis*, and this is where we get the word "dynamite." In the original Greek, it literally means "explosive, miraculous power."

I specifically remember one of these early experiences where I received prayer and fell under the power of the Holy Spirit. I was on the floor and shaking rather dramatically. It was so dramatic that I asked the Lord, "Lord, what is happening?" About that time, a lady leaned down and got near my face. I'm not sure where she came from, but I have to assume she was just nearby or walking by me as I lay on the floor. She whispered into my ear, "The Lord wants me to tell you that you are dining at His table."

I am immediately reminded of Psalm 23:5–6 (NLT), "You prepare a feast for me in the presence of my enemies. You honor me by anointing my head with oil. My cup overflows with blessings. Surely your goodness and unfailing love will pursue me all the days of my life, and I will live in the house of the Lord forever."

This encounter I had with the Lord took place in 2010, and I later discovered that in 2009, a leader in the Word of Faith movement also gave the following prophecy about "dining at the table of God"[2]:

> This is a feast of abundance in the valley of the shadow of death. Fear no evil! Fear not the shadow of death, not the valley therein. I, your Lord, your Savior—I am The LORD of hosts and I am the biggest thing in the valley. Have no fear for the table is full. Come and dine, come and dine. Pass the healing, pass the debt-free pudding. Yeah! Pass the miracles down here on this end of the table. Come and dine, come and dine.

Kenneth Copeland Ministries, KCM.org.

I traveled to Mobile and to that revival for about six months. I wasn't there every weekend, but I went as much as I could. I witnessed many miracles, signs, wonders, and healings. I made friends and quickly became part of what felt like a family of revival. It was the closest thing to "home" I had ever known, and that was one of the words the Lord spoke to me at that revival. He told me, "My presence is home." This made perfect sense. I had never been more aware of His presence than I had been during those months of revival. I felt at home in His presence, and I was comfortable and loved there. He went on to tell me that I was to forget about "home" being a place or a specific location. Home for me would now be where His presence was. I would also find His peace there. Home for me would no longer be a place but being in the center of His perfect will. That would be where I would find His presence and His perfect peace. These two things would now be what I valued most—His peace and His presence.

The Lord led the Israelites through the wildness using a cloud by day and a pillar of fire at night. We can see this in Exodus 13:

> The Lord went ahead of them. He guided them during the day with a pillar of cloud, and he provided light at night with a pillar of fire. This allowed them to travel by day or by night. And the Lord did not remove the pillar of cloud or pillar of fire from its place in front of the people.

Exodus 13:21–22 (NLT)

I felt the Lord was showing me this would be a picture of how He would lead me in the months and years to come. He was asking me to follow Him. I answered, "Here I am Lord, send me" (Isaiah 6:8).

Please pray with me.

Lord, thank You for revival. Please send revival! We need revival. Revive us, O Lord. Nothing else satisfies but You and Your presence. Your presence is literally heaven on earth. Your peace is invaluable. Masses of people and entire generations know entirely nothing about Your presence or Your peace, and they have found cheap substitutes to fill the incalculable void. Have mercy on us, Lord! We repent and turn from these cheap substitutes. We only want You, and nothing else will do. Please reveal Yourself to those who are lost and bound. You are the Creator of the heavens and the earth. You spoke and created it all, Lord. Set the captives free. Refresh and revive us. We are lost without You, but with You, all things are possible. We cry out for rescue and revival in the mighty name of Jesus!

Chapter 11: Prayer Changes Things

During my time at the farm, I watched a lot of Christian television, teaching, and preaching. One of my favorite Christian programs was a show that focused on the supernatural. A Jewish believer in Jesus hosted the show, and it ministered to me greatly. I found immense encouragement from watching it. Many of the guests would share their personal testimonies, and I could relate to so many of their stories. Their experiences often reminded me of my own, and that was also comforting and inspiring.

After months of watching this show, I began to notice a common thread in many of the guests. I kept hearing about a revival that had taken place in Pensacola, Florida. It was referred to as the "Brownsville Revival." In so many of the testimonies, I realized that a number had either visited this revival or had regularly visited in the nineties when it took place. These guests all had very similar testimonies. When they went to this revival, what they experienced there changed their lives and their ministries forever.

The Brownsville Revival, also known as the "Pensacola Outpouring," began on Father's Day, June 18, 1995, at the Brownsville Assembly of God in Pensacola, Florida. It is reported that more than 4 million people attended the revival meetings from its beginning in 1995 until around 2000.[3]

It became clear to me from watching so many testimonies about this revival that I needed revival as well. Since the Brownsville Revival was over, I began to pray for the Lord to send another revival. My prayer was simple and from the heart. If all the people I had seen on this show needed revival, then I needed revival too. I would pray,

3   "Brownsville Revival," Wikipedia, last modified July 4, 2021, https://en.wikipedia.org/wiki/Brownsville_Revival.

"Lord, send another Brownsville so I can go and receive all You have for me!"

In July 2010, the Lord called me to my first forty-day fast. I felt He was leading me to have one small meal a day and fast the remaining twenty-three hours. After forty days of fasting, I felt like I had really accomplished something in the Lord. It wasn't easy, but there was a grace on my fast that carried me through. Fasting is a powerful weapon in the Spirit, and I have seen fasting bring breakthrough and deliverance in my life over and over again.

Within a few days of finishing my fast, I was watching a Christian news program when they announced that a revival was taking place in Mobile, Alabama. The news anchor went on to report that this was the second revival for this pastor, who was also the pastor of the Brownsville Revival.

I was on the edge of my seat hearing and watching this and could hardly believe my ears and my eyes. My prayers had been answered! The Lord had sent revival again, and indeed, it would have to be similar to Brownsville with the same pastor. I made some calls and looked online and found that the revival had been going on for weeks. The following weekend I was in Mobile, Alabama. I had asked the Lord to send another Brownsville so that I could go and receive all He had for me, and He had done just that!

After months of traveling to revival, I didn't feel like the same person anymore. I was filled to overflowing with holy fire. I was "manifesting" the Holy Spirit in ways that were unfamiliar to me previously but were quite common in revival. In Romans 8, we see Paul speak of this:

> And in a similar way, the Holy Spirit takes hold of us in
> our human frailty to empower us in our weakness. For

example, at times we don't even know how to pray, or know the best things to ask for. But the Holy Spirit rises up within us to super-intercede on our behalf, pleading to God with emotional sighs too deep for words.

Romans 8:26 (TPT)

Indeed, what I was experiencing in revival was often "too deep for words."

Now, all I wanted to do was stay at revival and never leave, and I was beginning to sense the Lord was doing something new. I felt He was asking me to move to Alabama to be closer to revival and to be a part of what he was doing there. I had a deep desire to move, and I was more than willing to do it. I was ready.

I began to share this desire with some of the older and wiser women I had met at revival, and we began to pray into this move. Some of the women were really excited for me, and others were more cautious, but all were willing to pray for me. The more we prayed, the more excited I became, and I began to explore homes, jobs, and the details of actually making the move a reality.

On April 1, 2011, I left my hometown for the next adventure with the Lord. I moved into a condo in the beautiful bayside town of Fairhope, Alabama, on the eastern shore of Mobile Bay. Fairhope is the quintessential southern town complete with mossy-covered oaks and spectacular views of the bay. It always reminded me of stepping into a novel, back in time, or even the set of a movie. Fairhope was extraordinary, and I loved living there.

I found a job in sales and did well, but I did not like the long hours I was required to work or the fact that I often had to work on Sunday. The Lord performed a miracle, and within a few months, I was working from home for a Christian business. Working from home allowed me to spend more time with the Lord, and I felt more productive.

The revival that had gone on for many months was now all but over, but I was still deeply enjoying my church and gleaning so much from our pastor. I would spend the next two and half years in Alabama. It was a time of great spiritual growth for me and maturing. There was a lot of spiritual warfare, and there were a lot of spiritual victories.

In 2012, while living and working in Fairhope, I began to watch another Christian teacher and preacher on television. I had been watching this man for years, but now I found his teachings on grace to be life-changing. Often, I would find myself watching his broadcast multiple times a day.

I had been a Christian for several years at that time, and while my walk with the Lord had been miraculous and glorious, I need to be transparent and also say that it had not been easy. It felt like I was constantly facing battles on every front and the war being waged against me by the enemy was relentless. I found myself fighting weariness, fatigue, and even despair at times. I would find great comfort in 2 Corinthians 4:

> We are like common clay jars that carry this glorious treasure within, so that this immeasurable power will be seen as God's, not ours. Though we experience every kind of pressure, we're not crushed. At times we don't know what to do, but quitting is not an option. We are persecuted by others, but God has not forsaken us. We may be knocked down, but not out.
>
> 2 Corinthians 4:7–9 (TPT)

After years of walking with the Lord and seeing many miracles, signs, and wonders, I now found myself at either a breaking point or a tipping point.

Tipping point: (noun) the critical point in a situation, process, or system beyond which a significant and often unstoppable effect or change takes place.[4]

I was doing everything I was told, taught, and thought was expected of me to be a "good Christian," but I didn't feel like I was living or experiencing the victorious life the Lord had for me. Please don't misunderstand, my life was victorious, especially compared to the lifestyle and devastation I had walked out of, but I knew there was more. I had experienced revival and was now attending a vibrant, Bible-believing, devout church that valued holiness, revival, and the presence of the Holy Spirit; however, I was not experiencing the rest, ease, or peacefulness that I saw promised in the Bible. We can see this "rest" I so desperately needed and desired spoken of in the 11th chapter of Mathew:

> "Are you tired? Worn out? Burned out on religion? Come to me. Get away with me and you'll recover your life. I'll show you how to take a real rest. Walk with me and work with me—watch how I do it. Learn the unforced rhythms of grace. I won't lay anything heavy or ill-fitting on you. Keep company with me and you'll learn to live freely and lightly."

> Matthew 11:28–30 (MSG)

---

4   "Tipping point," Merriam-Webster, https://www.merriam-webster.com/dictionary/tipping%20point.

As I began to watch more teaching and preaching that focused on the grace of God, I also experienced more peace and more victory in my daily life. The ministry I had been watching multiple times a day was based in Colorado. They also had a Bible college called Charis Bible College. The name comes from the Greek word for "grace," which is *charis*.

At that point in my walk with the Lord, I had done multiple forty-day fasts, prayed daily, led a quiet life, did not date, attended church regularly, enjoyed a vibrant community of like-minded believers, loved the Lord, and worked from home for a Christian business. However, I was having migraine headaches, stomach ulcers, and also experiencing debilitating arthritis in my hands and wrist. I was also regularly fighting insomnia. I remember crying out to the Lord one day in a car with two older women. We were riding home from a prayer meeting, and I was asking them to pray for me. As I began to share with them my struggles and the battles I was fighting, I got really angry. I yelled out, "This is not a victorious life! God promises a victorious life, and this is not it! God, please help me! What is wrong?"

I'm not proud of yelling and being really angry, but I felt the Lord's pleasure in my being honest with Him in that moment. Somehow, I knew that because I had been honest with Him, He was going to be honest with me. I was mad because I was praying hours a day, fasting, and studying the Scriptures the best I knew how, but it felt like nothing was changing in my daily life. And many times, it felt like things were getting worse. I was also repenting at night for every imaginable sin I thought I had possibly committed, and still, I knew it was not enough. My mind was also a mess. I felt like I was constantly fighting negativity, bitterness, and unforgiveness.

I couldn't see that I was looking to all my "good works" as a means of salvation instead of looking to and resting in what Jesus had already done and accomplished for me. The Apostle Paul writes of this in Romans 10:

> I know what enthusiasm they have for God, but it is misdirected zeal. For they don't understand God's way of making people right with himself. Refusing to accept God's way, they cling to their own way of getting right with God by trying to keep the law. For Christ has already accomplished the purpose for which the law was given. As a result, all who believe in him are made right with God.
>
> Romans 10: 2–4 (NLT)

This is also seen in Isaiah 64:6 (NLT), "We are all infected and impure with sin. When we display our righteous deeds, they are nothing but filthy rags. Like autumn leaves, we wither and fall, and our sins sweep us away like the wind."

By relying on my own works, I had put myself under the law, and the Bible clearly says that anyone living under the law is also under a curse. Furthermore, I would also add that to try to live under the law is impossible for a mere human. It's impossible and endlessly frustrating.

> But those who depend on the law to make them right with God are under his curse, for the Scriptures say, "Cursed is everyone who does not observe and obey all the commands that are written in God's Book of the Law." So it is clear that no one can be made right with God by trying to keep the law. For the Scriptures say, "It

is through faith that a righteous person has life." This way of faith is very different from the way of the law, which says, "It is through obeying the law that a person has life." But Christ has rescued us from the curse pronounced by the law. When he was hung on the cross, he took upon himself the curse for our wrongdoing. For it is written in the Scriptures, "Cursed is everyone who is hung on a tree." Through Christ Jesus, God has blessed the Gentiles with the same blessing he promised to Abraham, so that we who are believers might receive the promised Holy Spirit through faith.

Galatians 3:10–14 (NLT)

I was beginning to grasp these truths in my life when I felt the Lord ask me to begin taking online Bible courses through Charis Bible College. I started by taking just two classes in my first quarter. I saw such improvement and breakthrough in my life that I took two more classes the following quarter. By the end of two quarters, I was fairly certain the Lord was calling me to move to Colorado and complete the Bible college in person on the main campus in Colorado Springs.

On December 12, 2012 (12/12/12), I received a phone call that only reaffirmed what I felt the Lord was speaking to me. A financial miracle took place that assured me the monetary means to move to Colorado, live there, and go to school. I felt like the Lord told me He had given me a "full-ride to Bible college."

I had indeed reached a "tipping point," and Colorado would prove to be a place of great convergence and breakthrough for me. Little did I know at the time of the financial miracle in December of 2012, but within four months, I would meet my future husband;

in about six months, I would be living in Colorado, and in less than nine months, I would be starting my second year of Bible college on campus at Charis in Colorado Springs.

The transition from Alabama to Colorado and all the months in between would not be easy, but they would be worth it. The Lord was teaching me how to enjoy the journey despite the contradictions and the spiritual warfare. When I think of that time, I am reminded of the famous lines from *A Tale of Two Cities* by Charles Dickens, "It was the best of times, it was the worst of times..." Indeed, it certainly felt that way, but a dream fulfilled is a tree of life! (Proverbs 13:12)

Please pray with me.

Father, thank You for being so faithful. When we cannot see, You are our eyes. Please give us greater discernment and increased and accurate spiritual vision to see things as You see them. Bring us teachers, pastors, and prophets who can speak accurately into our lives and help us to recognize blind spots. Thank You for increased revelation and wisdom. Your Word says to ask for wisdom, and You will supply it (James 1:5). Father, we ask for wisdom, and we need it. Please help us to be obedient, no matter the cost. Walking with You is not always easy, but it is worth it. Help us to recognize that it's the narrow path that leads to life, and although this path is difficult, help us to be among the few who do find it (Matthew 7:14). Help us to walk out the balance of this narrow life looking to You and the finished work of the cross and keeping our eyes off of our own "good works." We know the flesh profits nothing, but it is the Spirit that brings forth life (John 6:63). Thank You for bringing forth real life in us and transformation in Jesus' mighty name.

Chapter 12: The Mountains Are Calling

It was early spring 2013. I was on a plane looking out my window at the clear blue sky and feeling expectant and excited. Our plane was making its descent into Colorado Springs, Colorado. It was a cold day, but the sun was bright, and my heart was full. I had been waiting on this day for months, and it was finally here. I had been counting down the days like a child would do for Christmas.

I was on my way to visit Charis Bible College for the first time. I already felt I knew in my heart I was to go, but I knew the Lord was calling me to visit and see the campus for myself. Every spring, the school would host a three-day event called "Campus Days" and invite prospective students to visit the school and the campus. I was traveling there to do just that.

As the wheels went down and our plane landed, I was able to see the stunning range of mountains that ran through Colorado Springs from my window. I was stunned as I looked at the magnificent Rocky Mountains. *Those look like the mountains from my dream*, I exclaimed to myself! I had been to Colorado as a child many times, but I had never been to Colorado Springs. This was my first time seeing these mountains; however, when I saw them, I felt as if I had surely seen them before.

In a dream about a year and a half earlier, I had seen a similar range of mountains. This was no average dream. This was one of the most significant and encouraging dreams of my life. In the dream, I was shown my future husband. I had been living in Fairhope, Alabama, at the time of the dream, and moving to Colorado wasn't even on my radar. I knew very little of Charis Bible College and had no desire to move anywhere. In fact, at the time of the dream, I had only lived in Fairhope for a few months.

111

In my dream, I was looking at a couple standing in front of grand, snow-covered mountains. I was looking at them from behind, and they were holding hands. I could not see their faces, but I knew I was looking at myself and my future husband. He was quite tall, had a slim build, and a full head of dark hair. I am five foot four, and in the dream, my future husband seemed to tower above me. I woke up and could hardly believe what I had just experienced. *I just saw my husband,* I thought. *Wow! What did the mountains mean?* I wondered. *He's tall, and I'm sure he's handsome,* I thought. I relived that dream and pondered every detail of it over and over again.

I had been waiting for my future husband for years while I made the conscious choice to "wait and not date" in obedience to what I felt the Lord had shown me. When I went to Colorado for the first time, I was thirty-seven years old. I had been waiting about five years. Not dating in the thirties and then mid-to-late thirties wasn't easy. I found pressure from almost everyone to try and take matters in my own hands. Well-meaning Christians were always trying to be matchmakers. On several different occasions, these matchmakers even included their dreams, visions, and supposed "prophecies" from the Lord about men who they believed to be my "husband." None of these bore witness with me at the time, but they did cause a great deal of confusion.

In 2011, I received a prophecy from a trusted man I knew to be prophetically accurate. He had given me accurate prophecies in the past, and they had come to pass just as he had foretold. At a church service, he prophesied that I would meet my future husband in 2012 and went on to give specific details about him. This all bore witness with me, and I held on to that prophecy and told many people about it. I believed it would come to pass just as he foretold, but as 2012 was coming to a close, things began to look bleak. I truly held on and believed that I would meet my future husband even up until the last day of 2012. When the year was over, I was utterly devastated. I was also embarrassed because I had told so many people what I believed to be a true word from the Lord. I was also angry at this man for giving me an inaccurate prophecy.

I learned a lot from that painful lesson. I would now be very careful about receiving prophetic words from anyone, even trusted prophetic voices. After that experience, I began to pray into prophetic words I would receive and "put them on the shelf" if I was uncertain about them. I would also be more prayerful and wise about sharing my prophetic words with others, and I was learning for myself that prophecy with specific dates and times was rarely the Lord. I have personally found this to be true almost all the time. I do know the Lord can do whatever He wants and give times and dates if He chooses. I also know there is a biblical precedent in Scripture for this, but I have found for myself that He has almost never given me a prophecy that would turn out to be accurate if it had a time or date associated with it.

The disappointment of not meeting my mate in 2012 was very real, and it was devastating. My faith had been shaken, but in time, the Lord would heal me from that disappointment and renew my hope again. In fact, I would meet my future husband in late March of 2013—just a few months after the end of 2012. I believe the man who gave me that prophecy was hearing in part because his prophecy was close, but the date threw it off. He also gave me specific details in that prophecy about my husband that were actually true at that time. I believe He was picking up prophetically and did give me accurate details about my husband's life and even his personality. I forgave this man and released it all to the Lord. I know the Lord uses all things together for my good (Romans 8:28), and I believe it was true for this situation as well.

"And we know that God causes everything to work together for the good of those who love God and are called according to his purpose for them"

Romans 8:28, (NLT)

Being single in the church is not easy. The scriptures affirm this.

Two people are better than one, for they can help each other succeed. If one person falls, the other can reach out and help. But someone who falls alone is in real trouble. Likewise, two people lying close together can keep each other warm. But how can one be warm alone? A person standing alone can be attacked and defeated, but two can stand back-to-back and conquer. Three are even better, for a triple-braided cord is not easily broken.

Ecclesiastes 4:9–12 (NLT)

During my years of waiting, the Lord was doing great work in me to prepare me to be the wife I needed to be and also the mother I would become. This was not quick work. It was a work and a process that could not be rushed, and it is a work and a process that is ongoing. I found great comfort in knowing that Jesus was my husband even though I was single, and He was fighting for me and praying for me. I may have felt alone at times and fought feelings of loneliness, but I was not alone. I was also learning to trust Him.

"For your Creator will be your husband; the LORD of Heaven's Armies is his name! He is your Redeemer, the Holy One of Israel, the God of all the earth" (Isaiah 54:5, NLT).

Who then is left to condemn us? Certainly not Jesus, the Anointed One! For he gave his life for us, and even more than that, he has conquered death and is now risen, exalted, and enthroned by God at his right hand. So how could he possibly condemn us since he is continually praying for our triumph?

Romans 8:34 (TPT)

Jesus has proved Himself faithful time and time again. Truly, no one has been a better friend to me than Jesus. He told me He would bring my husband straight to me, and I would never have to date again, and He did just that. I believe He promised me I would have children (plural), and despite having them later in life, He kept that promise. I need to be transparent and tell you that this was not because I was always in faith. I fought discouragement at times and a lot of fear. I felt like I was always having to press through the voices telling me I would be an "old maid." I also had to counter the lies that told me even if I finally got married, I would have waited too long to have children. Basically, I fought those fears the entire time I was single and after I was married. All of those fears were based on lies. I found the truth in Psalm 113, "He gives the childless woman a family, making her a happy mother. Praise the Lord!" (Psalm 113:9, NLT) I saw the promise fulfilled when I held our first-born son in my arms. God is faithful!

But back in March of 2013, as I flew into Colorado Springs, I had not yet met my future husband, and the hope of children and a family of my own was still a dream in my heart. The next day as I visited Charis Bible College, a young man, who also happened to be tall, slim, and have dark hair, caught my eye. Later in the day, I found myself sitting a few rows behind him in a service the school was having for potential students. An instructor from the Bible college was speaking and stopped the service and began to speak to this young man. He told him to stand up, and the young man stood up. The instructor began to prophesy over him and gave a beautiful exhortation to him. As the young man stood in front of me and I heard what the Lord was prophesying over him and his destiny, I was overcome with a knowing in my heart that he was my future husband. Not only did he look like my husband from behind—just like the dream—but what was being spoken over him by the Spirit of the Lord was also confirmation. I felt in that moment that the Lord was telling me that this young man was indeed my future husband.

We would briefly meet and shake hands only once during this trip, but there was a knowing in my heart that it was already done. When it was time to return to Alabama, I wondered if and when our paths would cross again. We would meet again about five months later, in August of 2013. At that time, we would both be living in Colorado Springs and attending Bible college together. It was the beginning of something beautiful. Nine months later, we would be married.

If you are single, and even if you are married, and you are believing the Lord for things that look like they may never come to pass or facing insurmountable odds, I'm here to tell you that nothing is impossible with God (Matthew 19:26)! We serve a powerful God who wants to be involved in every detail of your life and show Himself strong on your behalf. If you are single, He is the mate you desire and need. If it is your heart's desire to be married, allow Him to do the work to prepare you and to do the work in your mate to prepare them. Be patient and know that our ways are not His ways (Isaiah 55:8).

"'My thoughts are nothing like your thoughts,' says the LORD. 'And my ways are far beyond anything you could imagine. For just as the heavens are higher than the earth, so my ways are higher than your ways and my thoughts higher than your thoughts'" (Isaiah 55:8–9, NLT).

I moved to Colorado and went to Bible college only because the Lord asked me to go. To be honest, I loved living on the Gulf Coast of Alabama. I thought it was one of the most beautiful places I had ever seen. I loved the mild winters and even the hot summers. On the other hand, Colorado was probably one of the last places I wanted to move to or live. I had no desire to live in that kind of climate, and I wasn't excited about the winters that lasted from November to June. I moved to Charis and went to Colorado only because I knew the Lord was calling me to do it. He gave me this scripture from Mark 10 to stand on as His promise to me:

> So Jesus answered and said, "Assuredly, I say to you, there is no one who has left house or brothers or sisters or father or mother or wife or children or lands, for My sake and the gospel's, who shall not receive a hundredfold now in this time—houses and brothers and sisters and mothers and children and lands, with persecutions—and in the age to come, eternal life."

> Mark 10:29–30 (NKJV)

It was all coming full circle. The first word the Lord gave me about my future husband was to seek first His Kingdom, and all these things would be added to me (Matthew 6:33). By "seeking first" His will and leaving what was comfortable and even more desirable for me, I found myself exactly where I was supposed to be. It was in that place that I found my future husband. I did not have to make it happen. It unfolded just as the Lord said it would, and there was an ease and a grace to it that was clearly supernatural. The Lord is a matchmaker, and He was making good on His promise.

I vividly remember leaving Colorado in March of 2013. I arrived back in Alabama to eighty-degree temperatures, and it felt almost like another world compared to what I had just left in Colorado. I was excited to visit Colorado, and now I also knew with certainty I was supposed to move there. This realization stirred new emotions in me. As I crossed the "Bayway," which is a seven-and-a-half-mile bridge that carries Interstate 10 across Mobile Bay, I was overcome with the absolute beauty of where I lived. The sun was setting, and the water reflected the glory of it all. I began to cry. "Lord, help me to leave. I know I am supposed to go. I want to go but help me to do it," I cried.

I would have to rely on a lesson I had been learning all along since I had given my life to Christ. From the very beginning, I was learning to die. Die, you may ask? Yes, die to self. You may have heard some Christians refer to this as "the way of the cross," as that is where Christ laid down His life for us. As Christians, we are also called to lay down our lives for Him. This is not a very popular message in some churches; nonetheless, it is what the Bible teaches.

> Then Jesus said to His disciples, "If you truly want to follow me, you should at once completely reject and disown your own life. And you must be willing to share my cross and experience it as your own, as you continually surrender to my ways. For if you choose self-sacrifice and lose your lives for my glory, you will continually discover true life. But if you choose to keep your lives for yourselves, you will forfeit what you try to keep. For even if you were to gain all the wealth and power of this world—at the cost of your own life—what good would that be? And what could be more valuable to you than your own soul?"
>
> Matthew 16:24–26 (TPT)

As I was leaving Colorado and waiting to board my flight, I felt the Lord speak to me about immediately beginning a forty-day fast. He used scripture to confirm what He was saying to me, and although I was not thrilled at first, I knew that if He was asking me to enter into this kind of fast, it was crucial. I said, "Yes, Lord." I'm glad I made the choice to follow the Lord and deny myself.

Please pray with me.

Father, we thank You for calling us up higher. Please give us the grace to trust You and Your ways even when it may not make sense or look possible. You are the God of the impossible. Jesus, You said, "... all things are possible to him who believes" (Mark 9:23, NKJV). We believe, Lord, help our unbelief! (Mark 9:24) Please give us the courage to stand when the world is telling us to sit down. Please give us the conviction to speak up when the world is telling us to keep quiet. Please give us the desire to wait when the world is pushing us towards instant gratification. As a Christian, the most important decision in life is the choice to follow Christ and make Him the Lord of your life. The next most important decision is the choice of who you will marry. Lord, we need You to move and help those seeking to find and fulfill Your best for them in their mate. Please expose deception and reveal truth to those desiring a true God-ordained marriage. Help them to keep their eyes on You and off of the detractions the enemy would bring to confuse and destroy. Expose the plots and plans of the enemy and strengthen those waiting with hope from heaven, divine dreams, and visions. Please make their paths straight and renew their strength as they wait (Isaiah 40:31). We also pray You would help us to choose the way of the cross and not our own desires when those desires don't line up with Your plans for our lives. We know that living a life for ourselves will not satisfy, and we ask that You would help us to continually live a life surrendered to Your will and Your ways. We pray all this in Jesus' mighty name. Amen.

Chapter 13: A Mile-High Life

Alabama is known as "Alabama, the Beautiful," and spring in Alabama certainly lives up to its name. To me, there was no other season that showcased the beauty of where I lived like spring. I knew I would get to enjoy one more spring before I moved to Colorado, and I was fully determined to do just that.

As I fasted and prayed, I also felt the Lord begin to speak to me about finishing up my first year of Bible college at that time so that I could begin as a second-year student when I began in Colorado in the fall. I doubled up on classes and added correspondence courses as well and finished my first year by mid-summer. During the fast, I also felt the Lord instruct me to make plans to move to Colorado earlier than I had originally planned. I knew He was telling me it was time to go.

On the final day of my forty-day fast, I had a dream and an experience that was monumental. It happened as I was awakening. I did not hear the audible voice of the Lord, but instead, I knew He was asking me the same question He asked Solomon. In the dream, I knew the Lord wanted me to ask for whatever I wanted, and I knew He was going to give it to me. It was very similar to Solomon's experience recorded in 2 Chronicles, "That night God appeared to Solomon and said, 'What do you want? Ask, and I will give it to you!'" (2 Chronicles 1:7, NLT)

I can remember this encounter and dream so vividly as if it had just happened. In the experience, I was overcome with a very real fear of the Lord. There was awe and wonder to it as well, but there was also a holy fear. I knew that I knew that the Lord was really going to give me whatever I asked for, and it felt more like an experience or an encounter than a dream. In this experience, I prayed, and I asked the Holy Spirit for wisdom to know how to answer. I prayed, "Holy Spirit, please help me to know what to ask for." I did not want to mess this up. I knew this was probably the most important question I would be asked in my entire life.

I then answered, "To love the Lord my God with all my heart, all my soul, and all my mind." As I finished my answer to the Lord, I woke up. It was the last day of my forty-day fast, and I could hardly believe what I had just experienced. I had given my answer straight from the Word of God. I thanked the Holy Spirit for giving me the wisdom to answer, and I was pleased with my request. I knew it would be done.

When asked by a religious scholar what the most important commandment was in the law of Moses, Jesus responded by saying:

> "'You must love the LORD your God with all your heart, all your soul, and all your mind.' This is the greatest commandment. A second is equally important: 'Love your neighbor as yourself.' The entire law and all the demands of the prophets are based on these two commandments."
>
> Matthew 22:37–40 (NLT)

Only the Holy Spirit could have helped me to answer so accurately. If Jesus said it was the most important commandment in the entire law, then I had to believe my request was received and accepted.

In the following weeks, I would fly to Colorado, find a condo, sign a lease, book a moving company and pack up my home. In early June 2013, I set out with Beazy and Bogey for a cross-country drive that would lead us to our new home in Colorado Springs. I was moved in and settled by mid-June and was there in time to enjoy a full summer in Colorado before school began in the fall. During that time, I was also able to continue working part time for the Christian business I had been working with in Alabama, as well as finishing up my first-year classes.

Before moving, I had been healed of the stomach ulcers I had been fighting for so many years, and I found that the migraines were significantly diminished and less frequent. I was also actively believing to be fully healed from the arthritis I was fighting in my hands and wrists. Some months earlier, I had been through some inner-healing and had prayed through forgiving and releasing some of the people from the past. It was at that point that all pain from ulcers completely vanished. I believe the bitterness and unforgiveness in my life had opened the door to the ulcers and the arthritis. The damage to my hands and wrists was notable. I could no longer open doors well, and I was not able to do push-ups anymore when I exercised. I was also dealing with pressure and pain in my hands all the time. Several people in my family suffered greatly from arthritis, and I believed that the enemy was also trying to bring this affliction on me. I also knew that Jesus Christ had redeemed me from the curse of arthritis, and by His stripes, I was already healed (1 Peter 2:24).

Charis Bible College hosts a weekly event called "Healing School." Here the faculty and students focus on teaching and demonstrating Biblical healing just as the Word of God promises. Almost immediately upon my arrival in Colorado Springs, I went to this "Healing School," expecting to be fully healed of arthritis and all the damaging effects it had on my body.

After the service, I went forward for prayer, and I found myself standing in front of an older man. He asked me, "What do you want God to do for you today?" I said, "I am going to receive my healing from all arthritis today, and I'm going to go home and do push-ups!" I had not been able to do pushups for probably a year, and I missed it. I was also mad that I was no longer able to carry bags of groceries or open doors without pain. I was only thirty-seven years old! I knew this was not my inheritance or my lot in life.

The man looked at me and with a big smile and said, "Amen! Well, let's pray." We began to pray and agree together for my healing. To be honest, I felt peace but not much else. It was not like revival where it felt like lightning bolts of holy fire were falling. It was just peaceful, and when we were done praying, I believed with all my heart I was healed. Nothing had changed that I could tell, but when I got home, I almost immediately got on the floor to do my first pushup. It was very painful. My wrist felt as if nothing had changed, but when I was done, I heard the Holy Spirit say, "Do it again." So I did it again. This time it was less painful. I could see there was progress. "Do it again," I heard. I did it again, and this time, it was significantly better. "Do it again," I heard once more. I did it again, and almost all the pain was gone. I began to run and jump through that condo like a little kid! I was overjoyed and beyond thankful! The next morning I felt I was supposed to try again, and when I did, there was absolutely no pain. I rejoiced and praised the Lord for the mighty miracle that had taken place. I was healed, and this was no small thing! Indeed, this was a notable miracle.

In the days and weeks that followed, I was amazed as "life before arthritis" returned. It was as if a decade or more of aging had been rolled back. The Lord had literally renewed my youth and restored my health. I had my life back, my hands back, my wrists back, and all the pain was gone. I was overjoyed and amazed as I was able to exercise again and do all the things I had stopped because of pain. No one but the Lord could have performed this kind of healing as well as the creative miracles it took to undo the damage to my joints and body. The healing was one miracle but restoring my body was another. I was so grateful, and I felt like I had a new lease on life. It was also a new beginning as I had only just moved to Colorado and had so much hope and expectation about what the Lord would do during my time there. I truly believed anything was possible.

During that first summer, I met several other students from Bible college and was enjoying new friendships. A new friend I had met contacted me shortly before classes were scheduled to begin. She mentioned that she had been speaking with some other students, and they were planning to meet for dinner at a local restaurant. She asked if I would like to come and meet some other students. I quickly said, "Yes!"

When I arrived at the restaurant, I sat down at a table with three other students from Charis. We all began to speak, and introductions were made. I noticed that two chairs were empty on the end of the table, so I thought maybe some other people might also be joining us. After a few minutes, I looked up, and standing above me was the handsome man I had seen a few months earlier, the young man I felt the Lord had highlighted as my future husband, and the man I wondered if I would ever see again. He sat down across from me at this table along with another student who came in with him, and I was hardly able to keep composure. "Lord, what are You doing?" I asked. I was left to draw my own conclusions, but it sure felt as if my first instincts might not be off.

We all enjoyed a meal as friends and had a wonderful time. I was able to visit with everyone, including the mystery man, and discovered his name was Aaron and that he was from West Virginia. He was kind, passionate about the Lord, and there was no pressure or awkwardness as we were all just friends enjoying the company of each other. There was also something very different about him that I found enormously attractive. He seemed very set apart from the world and the things of the world, and there was an innocence to him that was almost childlike. I found myself laughing and enjoying his company so much. Indeed, something unusual was most definitely taking place, and I felt the Lord in the midst of it all.

As school began, I continued to get together with small groups of friends that included different students from our school, and almost always, Aaron was there. I already felt I knew Aaron was my future husband, but I knew the Lord would have to do the work to tell him what He had already shown me. Supernatural things were also happening. It seemed like every time I turned around, I was running into Aaron at school. He was a first-year student, and I was a second-year student, so this wasn't impossible, but the likelihood that we would find ourselves together as often as we did was unusual. There were hundreds of students at Charis, but we would find ourselves "randomly together" in line over and over again. Driving to school, I almost always seemed to get either right behind Aaron or right in front of him on the interstate. We both had to jump on the interstate for a few miles to get to school, and somehow, we would be right there together multiple times a week, if not every day. After school, we would end up in line at the very same restaurant to have lunch, and then we would eat together. It was becoming almost embarrassing for us both. We each felt the need to state we were not intentionally following the other, but in fact, we both already knew that. Could it be that a heavenly agenda was playing out, and we were part of the plan?

As we got further into the fall, the weather began to change, and so did things between Aaron and me. It was clear that there was a great deal of spiritual warfare over us, and this was causing a very real struggle. The warfare was also bringing on some weariness. Despite everything I believed the Lord was showing me, I began to wonder and waver whether Aaron really was "the one." On a Friday afternoon, I left school and drove straight to Chick-fil-A for lunch. I went inside to eat by myself. I was relieved because I did not see Aaron's truck. If I had seen his truck, I would have left. I went inside, and as I walked in, I noticed that Aaron was there standing in line ordering. *What?* I thought! *How could this be?* I said to myself.

Aaron looked at me, and I could almost read his thoughts. They were the same as mine. I got behind him and said, "Hello." It was an awkward moment. I ordered my food, and while we waited, I asked him the obvious question. "Where is your truck? I did not see your truck," I said. He told me that he had parked on the other side of the building. We were beyond playing like we did not know something unusual was going on. "Oh! Well, I did not see it," I said. We sat down together to eat.

We enjoyed our meal and our time together, but I was growing tired of the status quo. When I got in my car, I resolved to do a three-day fast and not eat until Monday after school. I intended to hear from heaven for myself, and I believed the Lord was going to speak to me clearly and let me know for sure if Aaron was indeed my future husband. I knew something very supernatural was indeed playing out, and I wanted to partner with the Lord and clearly hear from Him on the matter.

I had learned for myself, and I had also been taught, that the spiritual discipline of fasting strengthens and helps you to walk by the Spirit so that you will not gratify the desires of the flesh (Galatians 5:16). Fasting had been a weapon I turned to over and over again to gain victory and breakthrough in my walk with the Lord. I knew we needed a breakthrough now, and I had waited too long for the promise to see the enemy steal it or me abort it because I got in the flesh or let my emotions get the better of me. I was deeply concerned of both.

I fasted all weekend, and on Monday, I returned to school, and it was the final hours of my fast. A woman who was older than me but in my class approached me. She said she had a word for me from the Lord. The Lord said, "You have favor with God, favor with man, and a good understanding." There was a weight to the word and specifically on the phrase "*a good understanding.*" I began to cry, and I hugged the woman. I felt the Lord was telling me that I indeed understood the situation, and I was also favored in it. I rested in that word, and what I felt the Lord had confirmed to me clearly. I believed Aaron was my future husband. I did not need to fear. I just needed to trust Him to bring it to pass. He would do it in His timing.

During my fast, I had also heard a phrase repeated several times in my spirit. I heard, "What you did not understand then, you will understand now." I heard this phrase whispered enough that I was expecting the Lord to reveal something new to me promptly. Just hours after breaking my fast, I was praying and worshipping in my bedroom when something dropped into my spirit.

While I was still living at the farm, I woke up on the morning of February 17, 2010, hearing "Exodus 30:8." This was no small thing at that time. I did not hear the audible voice of the Lord speak it, but it was strong enough that it almost felt like the audible voice of the Lord. I heard very clearly upon waking "Exodus 30:8." Although this was years earlier, I still remembered the event with clarity and conviction. It was definitely a word from the Lord, but at the time, in 2010, I had no idea what it meant. I sought out wisdom from older Christian women, but they were not sure what the Lord would be speaking to me either.

"And when Aaron sets up the lamps at twilight, he shall burn incense on it, a perpetual incense before the LORD throughout your generations" (Exodus 30:8, NKJV).

I studied out this scripture and meditated on it for a few weeks and then came back to it over and over again. I finally came to the conclusion that "incense" was symbolic of worship and that the Lord was speaking to me about praise and worship. I began to make praise and worship one of the last things I did before bed and the first thing I did when I woke in the mornings. This was the only conclusion I could come up with for this scripture, and to be honest, I was never satisfied that I had a full revelation of what the Lord was actually speaking to me. It always remained a bit of a mystery until that night in Colorado.

All of a sudden, while I was doing the very thing the scripture spoke of, revelation knowledge flooded me for the first time since I was given the scripture years earlier. Aaron's call, in part, is to worship. He has served in worship for over twenty years and has even served as a worship pastor in the past. He plays multiple instruments and has a beautiful voice and a pure heart of worship. The Lord had given me Aaron by name more than three years before I ever met him and even gave me clues about his call and our destiny.

"And when Aaron sets up the lamps at twilight, he shall burn incense on it, a perpetual incense before the LORD throughout your generations" (Exodus 30:8, NKJV).

Indeed, what I did not understand then, I understood now! I could hardly contain my excitement, and I erupted into spontaneous and uncontrollable praise! The Lord was speaking, and I was hearing His voice. My faith skyrocketed as I took in the enormity of it all.

I am reminded of Isaiah 46, "Remember the things I have done in the past. For I alone am God! I am God, and there is none like me. Only I can tell you the future before it even happens. Everything I plan will come to pass, for I do whatever I wish" (Isaiah 46:9–10, NLT). Amen and amen.

I was certain it was done. Now, I needed to wait, as I knew the Lord would have to speak to Aaron about what He had shown me. In the following weeks, Aaron and I would continue our friendship. We began talking on the phone at night, and those conversations would last for hours. We were getting to know each other, and I loved being with him. I loved talking with him, and I felt so safe with him. As his friend initially, I was able to see the fruit in his life without the pressure, trappings, and temptations of dating. There was so much I loved about Aaron and admired about his walk with the Lord. Our relationship was built on the foundation of a friendship first and the Lord foremost. I could see the hand of God in every detail of the story He was writing, and I was certain this story was already written. It was a really beautiful time, and we were still just friends, although I felt as if I already loved him. I had been waiting for this my entire life.

Please pray with me.

Father, we thank You that You can tell us the future before it even happens. Nothing is too hard for You. You deserve all the praise and all the glory. You are good, and You are even better than we know! You are a Father to the fatherless, and You place the lonely in families (Psalm 68:5–6). Hallelujah! We pray for everyone reading this book who is single and longing to find their godly mate. We decree that You will surely bless the righteous and Your favor surrounds them like a shield (Psalm 5:12). Father, we know that preparation time is never wasted time. Help each one of Your children to do the work to prepare themselves for marriage. For some, it may be going to Bible college, or others may need to receive healing in their hearts and souls. Whatever is needed, please give them the grace to prepare themselves to be the healthy and whole person You need them to be. Some may simply need to be patient and wait. This often is not easy and requires taking up one's cross daily and dying to self. Please help them to do it. The world celebrates instant gratification, but it's an anomaly in the Kingdom of God. We pray for truth, wisdom, and understanding, and for Your perfect will to come to pass in our lives. In Jesus' mighty name. Amen.

Chapter 14: Beauty for Ashes

It was mid-November in Colorado, and there was a chill in the air. The colorful show the trees had displayed for fall was over, and the Aspens were bare. Fall was beginning to make way for winter.

It was Sunday morning, and I was in church by myself when I noticed Aaron come in and sit a few rows in front of me. After church, he sent me a text and asked if I would have time to talk with him later in the evening on the phone. I told him, "Yes," and waited for his call. Somehow, I knew this call was going to be different. I tried to prepare myself, but fear got the best of me during those final hours of waiting. Instead of believing for the best, I was honestly concerned that the worst would unfold. I was a wreck by the time the phone rang that night.

He was kind, and we chitchatted for a few minutes before he began to speak about what was really on his heart. He began by first apologizing if the conversation was awkward or if he was in any way making me feel uncomfortable. Then he said, "I think the Lord may be speaking, and He's speaking to me about us. Is the Lord showing you anything about us?"

I sat there a few moments as I tried to gain my composure and speak what the Lord would have me to speak, but I was ready to burst and yell it from the mountain tops. "Yes," I said calmly. "I believe the Lord has been speaking to me about 'us.'"

Aaron went on to share how he believed the Lord was bringing us together as a couple. I told him I agreed wholeheartedly. We revisited so many of the supernatural situations that unfolded during the fall and our time together as friends and felt the Lord was leading us to each other. We both knew this was not just to "date." We both felt the Lord had shown us that we were to be married.

I told him about my dream where I felt I was shown my future husband standing with me in front of snow-covered mountains and how I believed it was him in the dream. I also told him about Exodus 30:8 and that I believed the Lord gave me "Aaron" by name more than three years earlier. He was encouraged, and I was greatly comforted.

As the conversation unfolded, I was reminded of what the Lord had spoken to me so many years before. I was told that if I would wait and not date, He would bring my mate straight to me. He had done just that. I had never been on a date with Aaron; we were only friends. But here we were, speaking of marriage and life as if it had already happened and was, in fact, done. We spoke for hours that night, and before we got off the phone, he laughed and suggested that if we were to be married, we might want to go out on a date soon. I agreed that would probably be a good idea. He asked me to go out to dinner with him the following Friday night and to see a movie. I said, "Yes."

It was official. After years of waiting and not dating, I was going on my first date with the man I believed would be my future husband. The Lord was fulfilling His word and His promises. I went to bed overjoyed and could hardly sleep. At times I had fought so much discouragement and fear waiting during those years, but now, here I was, stepping into the promise and blessing the Lord had pledged. It reminded me of Proverbs 13:12 (TPT), "When hope's dream seems to drag on and on, the delay can be depressing. But when at last your dream comes true, life's sweetness will satisfy your soul."

My soul certainly felt satisfied. I had so much peace and joy I could hardly contain myself. When I woke the following morning, Colorado Springs had turned into a winter wonderland. A beautiful blanket of fresh snow covered the ground. It was the first real snow of the season, and it felt like another world. Aaron called to see if I needed help getting to school in the snow. I told him I thought I would be just fine. It turned out my two-wheel-drive convertible wasn't made for Colorado winters, and I called him from the side of the road a few minutes later. I really enjoyed being rescued by him that day.

We drove into school together for the first time and sat together in the chapel. I was in love, and my heart was so full. I felt as if anything was possible, and I knew my best days were in front of me. I can instantly visualize a dozen or more glorious images and memories from my born-again life that are awe-inspiring and display the goodness of God, and in reality, there are hundreds more. But this memory is among one of my most favorites. It was the first day of my new life with Aaron. We were a couple. This was "us," and life as "us" was just beginning.

When I look back and realize that before Jesus, there was a night in my life that I was ready to die, it almost doesn't seem possible now. But back then, before Jesus, I was blind. I could not see the future God had planned for me. I could not see this moment in Colorado with my future husband. The devil did not steal it, and he did not steal my life from me. I'm still here. God in His mercy preserved my life from destruction. My life is amazing. My life is glorious, miraculous, and my life is His. He saved my life, and I have given my life back to Him.

I can't help but think of the hymn, "Jesus Paid It All."

> I hear the Savior say,
>
> "Thy strength indeed is small;
>
> Child of weakness, watch and pray,

Find in Me thine all and all."

Refrain:

Jesus paid it all;

All to Him I owe;

Sin had left a crimson stain,

He washed it white as snow...

Snow. A fresh blanket of snow can make almost anything look magical. As we walked out of school together that first time as a couple, we looked at Pike's Peak covered in snow. Pike's Peak is the highest summit of the southern Front Range Rocky Mountains, and it is a sight to behold on any day. But on this day, it was particularly majestic. Snow was everywhere we looked, and by midday, the sun was reflecting and shimmering in it. I was reminded of what the psalmist penned in Psalm 118. "This is the LORD's doing, and it is wonderful to see. This is the day the LORD has made. We will rejoice and be glad in it" (Psalm 118:23–24, NLT).

Please pray with me.

Father, You amaze us. You are amazing. You created the mountains and the seas. You created it all, and Your creation is amazing. To enjoy creation without enjoying the Creator is to miss the mark. When I look back at my life and think of all the years I lived without real knowledge or relationship with You, I am almost undone. I can't make it a moment without You now. How did I make it all those years? The answer is I did not make it all those years without You because You were with me through it all. You have always been there, and You always will be. Your Word says You will never leave us or forsake us (Hebrews 13:5). Thank You for not leaving us. Thank You for rescuing us over and over again. Thank You for second chances. Thank You, Jesus, for the cross and making a way where there was no way. You took back what was stolen, and You have never stopped redeeming and restoring. You alone, Lord, can make all things new (Revelation 21:5). Thank You for making all things new in our lives as we surrender them to You. Please help us to surrender and empower us with Your grace to run the race You have for us. We want to hear, "Well done, good and faithful servant" (Matthew 25:21). In Jesus' mighty name. Amen.

Chapter 15: Two Becoming One

As November was coming to an end, the Christmas season was just beginning. Many of our classmates were leaving to travel back home, and Aaron was packing up to be back in West Virginia by Thanksgiving. I had planned on staying in Colorado for Thanksgiving and through much of December. I would travel to the North Carolina Mountains to spend the holiday with my family just a few days prior to Christmas.

It is said that "absence makes the heart grow fonder," but I couldn't imagine that even being possible until after Aaron left. My heart was already so full, and the short time we had spent together had only reaffirmed what we felt we already knew about each other. Yes, we were discovering that the Lord certainly knows how to be a divine matchmaker. I had never in my entire life felt anything close to what I was experiencing with Aaron. Before Jesus, I had experienced dating and felt I knew what love was, but I can tell you nothing came even close to what I was experiencing with Aaron. This was the kind of love I had waited my entire life to find, and it was not just any kind of love. It was a divine love with Jesus Christ in the center of it all. It was supernatural, and it was altogether wonderful.

I could not help but think back on my experience that fateful afternoon on the island of St. Maarten over a decade earlier. The Lord had given me a glimpse of what He wanted to give me. It was a love like no other. It was a love I couldn't even comprehend at that time, but it was mine if I would only open my heart to what the Lord wanted to do and what He wanted to give me. That love was found in Him because God is love (1 John 4:8), but I would also find that love in the gift of Aaron.

As the weeks began to pass, we were searching for a way to see each other. His hometown was just a few hours from our family's home in North Carolina. It was decided that he would drive to visit and meet my family in North Carolina after Christmas, and I would drive back with him to his hometown. I would then meet his family and spend some time with them in West Virginia.

Aaron and I each came from extraordinarily different backgrounds. I grew up in a secular home with a privileged life. Aaron grew up in a devout Christian home with very little influence from the world and a very modest lifestyle. However, we both grew up in small towns, and we could relate to small-town life. Aaron was homeschooled his entire life, saved at an early age, and baptized at six years old. Aaron doesn't drink; in fact, he has never had a sip of alcohol his entire life and has always pursued a passionate relationship with the Lord.

My life before Jesus was almost the opposite of his. To be honest, I always thought the Lord would match me with someone who came out of addiction like I did or had a similar background, but this was not His plan for me. He matched me with someone who had lived one of the most pure and devoted lives in Christ I could possibly find. This was and still is deeply humbling for me. I am so grateful the Lord picked Aaron to be my husband. His pure life and level of sanctification were a perfect match for the work the Lord had done to prepare me to be his wife.

According to Easton's 1897 Bible Dictionary:

> Sanctification involves more than a mere moral reformation of character, brought about by the power of truth: it is the work of the Holy Spirit bringing the whole nature more and more under the influences of the new gracious principles implanted in the soul in regeneration. In other words, sanctification is the carrying on to

perfection the work begun in regeneration, and it extends to the whole man.

In all my years of waiting, I often prayed to the Lord and expressed my concerns about my own level of sanctification. I knew it was a good thing to be "set apart in Christ," but at times, I wondered if I would ever find anyone who would understand the level of sanctification the Lord had called me to walk in. This was yet another lie of the enemy. The scriptures speak a better word.

"You have been set apart as holy to the LORD your God, and he has chosen you from all the nations of the earth to be his own special treasure" (Deuteronomy 14:2, NLT).

"Stop imitating the ideals and opinions of the culture around you, but be inwardly transformed by the Holy Spirit through a total reformation of how you think. This will empower you to discern God's will as you live a beautiful life, satisfying and perfect in his eyes" (Romans 12:2, TPT).

> Don't set the affections of your heart on this world or in loving the things of the world. The love of the Father and the love of the world are incompatible. For all that the world can offer us—the gratification of our flesh, the allurement of the things of the world, and the obsession with status and importance—none of these things come from the Father but from the world. This world and its desires are in the process of passing away, but those who love to do the will of God live forever.
>
> 1 John 2:15–17 (TPT)

Then there was also the issue of age, which really is no issue at all, but I had made a molehill into a mountain. I discovered shortly after meeting and getting to know Aaron that he was almost ten years younger than me. This was shocking at first because I thought he was older than he actually was. It was during our monumental phone call where we shared the truth about what we felt the Lord was showing us that I shared my age. He admitted he thought I was younger but was honest in explaining that all his life, he has always found his closest friends to be around ten years older than him. It was no big deal to him. It was normal.

The Lord had actually taken me through a process of being prepared for the age difference. During the forty-day fast I had completed just before moving to Colorado, the Lord spoke to me quite clearly about age not being an issue in the Kingdom of God. I felt He spoke quite clearly that age is an issue in the world. I then was led to research great men and women of God through the years. I was specifically looking at their spouses. During my research, I found multiple examples of couples that had differences in their age and were great leaders in the body of Christ during their generation. I had even read a book by Derek Prince titled *God is a Matchmaker,* which had a profound impact on me. I also believe the Lord gave me His divine blueprint for God-ordained marriage through that book. Derek Prince wrote about his first wife, Lydia, and their age difference. In fact, in the book, he states that she was "considerably older." *What is considerably older?* I thought. I began to research their marriage and indeed found that she was almost twenty-five years older. Lydia Prince went on to be with Lord, and Derek Prince would later remarry, but I was getting the point. Age is a non-issue to the Lord. He wanted me to make it a non-issue as well.

My own insecurities made that harder than it needed to be, but since it appeared to be of no significance to Aaron, I tried to let it go as well. We honestly looked close in age, and we did not feel or notice the age difference unless we focused on it, so it eventually became of little or no importance to us both. I was learning to let go of the world's influence so that I could be influenced by the only One that matters. Now, I really appreciate and love the difference in age, as I see it as just another creative way the Lord has given me back some of the years the enemy attempted to steal. It's a promise declared in Joel 2, "So I will restore to you the years that the swarming locus has eaten...You shall eat in plenty and be satisfied, And praise the name of the LORD your God, Who has dealt wondrously with you; And My people shall never be put to shame" (Joel 2:25–26, NKJV).

The meeting of parents was surreal. It was even more evident being together in the homes our parents owned how different our lives were. I want to be transparent because I believe my transparency will be both a blessing and an encouragement to other couples facing similar circumstances. The Lord's main focus isn't on your background or your parent's cultural preferences, as much as He is focused on where you are going. He places couples together and sees their future, their children, and the plans He has for them. He also sees multi-generationally, as He is the God of Abraham, Isaac, and Jacob (Matthew 22:32). He sees your grandchildren and your great-grandchildren. Man may want to look back, but the Lord is asking man to look forward. Despite the differences, we both knew that the Lord had placed us together for a divine purpose. We believed that with all our hearts, and we were committed.

On February 21, 2014, Aaron asked me to marry him. I said, "Yes!" Four months later, on June 14, 2014, we were married in the North Carolina Mountains. Our small family wedding was beautiful and special. We did our best to keep Jesus at the center of our wedding and our wedding night. I can tell you that waiting to be intimate on your wedding night is well worth the wait. We waited, and it was worth it. Nothing compares to keeping purity and Jesus in the center of your world, your wedding, and your wedding night.

We are instructed in Scripture to lead pure lives, and this includes abstaining from immorality. Unfortunately, the American culture and mass media as a whole promote immorality and often paint a vile and perverse picture of love and what love looks like. If you are coming out of the world, I urge you to read what the Bible has to say about the truth and let that truth set you free. How do I know these things? Because I was once blind, and now I see. I was once indoctrinated into the world and its lusts and covered in sin and shame. I was part of the walking dead. No, I'm not talking about the television series—I'm talking about being a "walking dead man" out in the world. That may be who I was, but that is not who I am. Jesus has set me free, and who the Son sets free is free indeed (John 8:36). I am now a citizen of heaven (Philippians 3:20). I am now a child of God (1 John 3:10), and I will live forever (John 6:51). He wants to do the same thing for you.

> Run from sexual sin! No other sin so clearly affects the body as this one does. For sexual immorality is a sin against your own body. Don't you realize that your body is the temple of the Holy Spirit, who lives in you and was given to you by God? You do not belong to yourself, for God bought you with a high price. So you must honor God with your body.
>
> 1 Corinthians 6:18–20 (NLT)

"Honor the sanctity of marriage and keep your vows of purity to one another, for God will judge sexual immorality in any form, whether single or married." (Hebrews 13:4, TPT).

> God's will is for you to be set apart for Him in holiness and that you keep yourselves unpolluted from sexual defilement. Yes, each of you must guard your sexual purity with holiness and dignity, not yielding to lustful passions like those who don't know God. Never take selfish advantage of a brother or sister in this matter, for we've already told you and solemnly warned you that the Lord is the avenger in all these things. For God's call on our lives is not to a life of compromise and perversion but to a life surrounded in holiness. Therefore, whoever rejects this instruction isn't rejecting human authority but God himself, who gives us his precious gift—his Spirit of holiness.
>
> 1 Thessalonians 4:3–8 (TPT)

If you, like me, know the pain of not walking in this purity—purity that is a free gift that comes with salvation in Jesus Christ—I urge you to make the choice to begin walking in it today. John, the "beloved," wrote, "But if we freely admit our sins when his light uncovers them, he will be faithful to forgive us every time. God is just to forgive us our sins because of Christ, and he will continue to cleanse us from all unrighteousness" (1 John 1:9, TPT).

I believe the Lord is calling many of you to come up to a higher level, and I believe today can be your day of breakthrough and salvation.

"As God's partners, we beg you not to accept this marvelous gift of God's kindness and then ignore it. For God says, 'At just the right time, I heard you. On the day of salvation, I helped you.' Indeed, the 'right time' is now. Today is the day of salvation" (2 Corinthians 6:1–2, NLT)

Please pray with me.

Jesus, thank You for the gift of purity You have given us. We ask You to please forgive us for where our lives have missed the mark. We repent of any time we have chosen immorality over Your Word and Your ways. Please forgive us. You are pure, and Your blood has washed us whiter than snow (Psalm 51:7). Help us to walk out this purity by choosing to honor Your Word and Your truth over feelings, emotions, and what the world would tell us. Thank You for calling those You have chosen back to You. You have asked us to forsake the world and its ways to walk surrendered lives in You. This call will not be easy, and it will cost some everything, but it will be worth it. There is no way to walk out the real Christian life without You. We are not talking about the "cheap Christian life," we are talking about the costly Christian life. The life that looks, talks, and walks differently than the world. The life that walks in resurrection life and power. This is the life we are talking about, and this is the life we want to live. We want to walk out this kind of life with You, and we want to see heaven invade earth. There is no way to walk in that kind of power by living halfway in the world and walking in compromise. We know that what a person is willing to compromise, they will eventually lose. Help us to walk out a life without compromise and see the billion-soul harvest come now into Your Kingdom. We decree and declare that we are overcomers, and we overcome by the blood of the Lamb and the word of our testimony (Revelation 12:11). Let Your Kingdom come and Your will be done on earth as it is in heaven (Matthew 6:10). In Jesus' mighty name. Amen.

Chapter 16: "I Set Before You Life and Death—Choose Life."

The year 2014 was a year filled with promise and blessing. In May of 2014, I graduated from Charis Bible College with a master's degree in Biblical Studies. It seemed almost providential that I graduated from Charis twenty years after my high school graduation. I had graduated from high school in June of 1994 and followed the same path my parents had taken and graduated from their alma mater, the University of Georgia. Now it felt like I was getting a second chance to do it all over again and follow the path my heavenly Father had laid out for me.

In June, Aaron and I were married, and the summer of 2014 was a time of adjustment as we were learning to become one. Our first few married months were both wonderful and challenging. We are both strong-willed, and while it serves each of us well as we stand for Christ, it was also a character trait that was causing conflict in our marriage. We were learning to adjust to life as a couple and leave a lot of baggage from our past behind. We had to navigate many trials and storms that were self-inflicted because of selfishness and personality conflicts. We were proactive in doing premarital counseling, we took courses in school on marriage, we read books on love and biblical marriage, but we were still struggling and often found ourselves at odds with each other. At the same time, we were also still very much in love, and we could feel the Lord's grace and mercy flood our marriage. He was helping us press through and carrying us through every painful situation. We learned a lot of lessons, never stopped praying, got help when we needed it, and slowly our marriage began to turn around.

In the fall, Aaron started his second year of Bible college, and I began a third-year program at Charis in the field of media. It was wonderful being back in school together. We were indeed learning to become one, and we were settling into married life. In late December, just a few days before Christmas, I found out I was pregnant. It was one of the most wonderful and amazing moments of my life. I had prayed and believed the Lord for a godly husband, and He had given me Aaron, and we had been praying for this child. I am reminded of Hannah, who, after receiving the long-awaited promise of a child, gives the young boy back to the Lord. "'For this child I prayed, and the Lord has granted me my petition which I asked of Him. Therefore I also have lent him to the LORD; as long as he lives he shall be lent to the LORD.' So they worshiped the LORD there" (1 Samuel 1:27–28, NKJV).

I wasn't prepared for how sick I would be the first few months of the pregnancy and how hard that would prove to be at times. Not only did I lose weight, but I actually had to stop going to school for a period of time. I found out a fiery evangelist from Mexico known to move in mighty signs and wonders was visiting the Bible college and would be ministering at the Healing School. I knew I had to go. I had been praying to be healed of all "morning sickness," but I still was feeling terrible. I also wasn't sure why they called it "morning sickness." I was sick morning, noon, and night.

I went to the healing service believing to be healed and delivered. The evangelist preached and taught, but mostly, he prayed for people by the laying on of hands. Almost every person he prayed for had some reaction to the Holy Spirit that could be visibly seen. Some were explosive, and some were less, but all were obviously being touched by the Holy Spirit. Most people just fell to the ground, and as he began to make his way to me, I wondered how this would work being pregnant. I wasn't new to this after all the time I spent in revival, but I wasn't pregnant then, and I did not want to fall. He placed his hand on my head and called for "fire." At that exact moment, I felt what I can only describe as a bolt of power come through my head down my body and into my womb. I knew at the exact moment it happened that the prayer may have been for me, but the power went into our baby. I gently fell back into my chair and sat there covered and surrounded by the peace and presence of God. I can't remember feeling sick, but I do remember feeling such peace and joy about what had just taken place.

After the service, I went back home and asked the Lord about what had taken place. I felt the Lord showed me He had actually touched our son with the fire of God even before birth. I had experienced a baptism of fire in revival, but I felt He was telling me He had baptized our son with the Holy Spirit and with fire in the womb. I found this clearly demonstrated in the gospel of Matthew. "I baptize with water those who repent of their sins and turn to God. But someone is coming soon who is greater than I am—so much greater that I'm not worthy even to be his slave and carry his sandals. He will baptize you with the Holy Spirit and with fire" (Matthew 3:11, NLT).

Later, this was confirmed when I returned to school and received a prophecy about our son from a friend. One of the most wonderful things about being pregnant in Bible college was all the prayer. So many people wanted to pray for our baby and me, and I loved it. I received so many wonderful prophecies about our family, our children, and our future. I would record and keep most of them, but this one was of particular importance because it confirmed a sign and a wonder that I had witnessed and been a part of in our son's life.

At the same time, I was fighting a great deal of fear throughout most of my pregnancy. I prayed and knew the Word. I knew that faith empowered God and fear did the same thing to the enemy, but it continued to be something I had to press through during most of my pregnancy. I knew that God had not given me the spirit of fear but of power, love, and a sound mind (2 Timothy 1:7), but walking that out seemed to prove so much more difficult than it needed to be. At times, I was riddled with paralyzing and irrational fear. I was so scared that after waiting forty years to be a mother, I would lose the promise after being so close to seeing it come to pass. I was scared that I would somehow mess it up or eat the wrong thing or say the wrong thing. I was just scared. I knew I was not supposed to be afraid, but I fought so much fear. As the baby grew and began moving, I was comforted by feeling him move, but then I was frightened if I did not feel him move, and on and on it went. The Scriptures say, "fear has torment," and it is the truth. "There is no fear in love; but perfect love casts out fear, because fear involves torment. But he who fears has not been made perfect in love. We love Him because He first loved us" (1 John 4:18–19, NKJV).

I was fighting a great deal of anxiety and worry one morning at Bible college when one of my classmates approached me and asked if she could pray for me. I was more than willing and so grateful that she wanted to pray for me. She and her husband had come from the UK with their son to Bible college. They were passionate and on fire for the Lord. She began to pray for me and spoke to the fear, and commanded it to go. A wave of deep peace came over me, and then she began to pray for our baby. She prayed for the pregnancy and began to prophesy over our son's life. She specifically said that he would be like John the Baptist and be baptized and filled with the Holy Spirit even while in the womb. This is mentioned in Luke 1.

> "Many will rejoice because of him, and he will be one of
> the great ones in the sight of God. He will drink no wine

or strong drink, but he will be filled with the Holy Spirit
even while still in his mother's womb"

Luke 1:14–15, TPT

I began feeling better and standing against fear around the
halfway mark of my second trimester. I began to gain some weight
and experience the joy of being pregnant. It was around this time that
I truly discovered the absolute joy of every kick and every moment
of pregnancy. The fear and the sickness wanted to rob me of this, but
the joy was now bubbling over. I felt so beautiful being pregnant, and
I began to truly enjoy it. As the end of the school year was nearing,
preparations were being made for graduation. Aaron was graduating
from the two-year program, and I was graduating from the third-
year program. I was asked to speak at graduation and represent the
Media School. I was six months pregnant as I walked across the stage
to receive my diploma and to speak. It is one of the most beautiful
and treasured of all my memories. A picture of the goodness, grace,
faithfulness, and great mercy of our awesome God. I was pregnant
with our son, but I also felt I was pregnant and bursting with destiny.
My charge to my classmates was simple: "Let's go change the world."

During the second half of my pregnancy, I went through a process
that shifted so much of how I processed life. As Daniel grew and
kicked and moved, I was moved with great love and compassion for
him and the unborn. It is difficult for me to imagine how any woman
carrying a baby and watching and feeling that baby grow would not
know the humanity of that child and have great compassion for it. It
was during this time in my pregnancy that undercover videos emerged
that appeared to reveal the selling and trafficking of baby body parts
by the nation's largest abortion provider. This was national news and

I was so outraged, horrified, and even somewhat traumatized by this. I lay in bed at night, trying to wrap my head around how this was happening in our country. I woke up in the night thinking about it and found myself crying out to the Lord in prayer daily about it.

I was at another tipping point in my life. Before Christ, I would have said I was "pro-choice." I bought the lie the world sells that convenience makes it okay to kill. I bought the lie that if you abort a baby early enough, it's really not a baby, and it certainly couldn't hurt. I did not know the biblical truths that counter the lies, and so I believed them. After I was saved, the Lord began to deal with me on abortion and other biblical issues that are near to His heart. He showed me the truth, and although it did not happen all at once or overnight, I let go of a lifetime of indoctrination in the world's system. One by one, the lies that I had been sold as truth were dismantled, uprooted, removed, and replaced with the truth. Abortion was one of them. But I have to be honest; I was not passionately pro-life. I knew it was wrong, but it did not keep me up at night.

All of that changed while I was pregnant with Daniel. I was gripped with the realization that my precious son was legal to kill in all fifty states and that thousands of innocent babies like him were being dismembered and brutally murdered in their own mother's womb every day. At times it felt as if it was almost too much to bear, but the Lord showed me how to cast my cares on Him (1 Peter 5:7)— through prayer and trusting Him. I believe He personally showed me that abortion would be abolished in America. Please hear me; it is not a matter of if it will happen but when it will happen. Slavery was an abomination to the Lord and to a large segment of the population, but it was still fiercely fought for because of cultural ignorance and economic greed. The same thing is happening today with abortion and the billions of dollars generated by it. The Lord is calling the body of Christ to wake up and stand up for those who cannot speak for themselves. It is my heartfelt prayer that every person reading this book becomes a passionate advocate for every unborn child waiting to fulfill their destiny and find themselves on the right side of history.

"Speak up for those who cannot speak for themselves; ensure justice for those being crushed. Yes, speak up for the poor and helpless, and see that they get justice" (Proverbs 31:8–9, NLT).

In August, I turned forty years old. I was nine months pregnant and waiting for Daniel to arrive. It was a milestone birthday, and I can tell you honestly that turning forty was wonderful. I felt like my best days were right in front of me, and I believed anything was possible. I am reminded of Haggai 2:9, and I particularly love the Message translation, "'This Temple is going to end up far better than it started out, a glorious beginning but an even more glorious finish; a place in which I will hand out wholeness and holiness.' Decree of GOD-of-the-Angel-Armies" (Haggai 2:9, MSG).

On August 25, 2015—ten days after my fortieth birthday—Daniel Aaron Butte was born weighing eight pounds and four ounces. He was the most beautiful thing I had ever seen, and at times, I literally thought my heart would burst with pride and love. The first few weeks and months at home with our newborn were so innocent, extraordinary, and even heavenly. It was such a special time, and it felt as if we were often living under an open heaven. We would often catch Daniel smiling, giggling, or gazing at the ceiling and interacting with what appeared to be nothing to us, but it was something to him. This became so commonplace that it was just assumed that we were not alone.

I remember on a particular night around three in the morning, I was in Daniel's room feeding him, and I was overcome with emotion and a deep, intimate love. As I looked into his eyes—he now has brown eyes, but then they were still a beautiful shade of blue—I had one of the most dreamlike but real of experiences. As I looked into his eyes, I was undone. I do not know how to describe in human or earthly words what I saw that would do it justice, but the closest thing I can imagine is that I saw heaven in a moment in my son's eyes. I began to weep from a deep, deep place in me and the love that overcame me was a love that was unfathomable. It swept over us both as I held Daniel as a newborn baby in my arms, and it wrapped us up together. Tears were now streaming down my face and onto him, and all I could do was hold on to him as I felt the Lord hold on to us both. What love He has for us! I was given a glimpse of that love in a moment, and I felt like my heart could not contain it, nor my soul hold it. I was utterly and completely undone.

Aaron went back to Charis to complete his third year shortly after Daniel was born. I stayed home with Daniel during that year while Aaron finished. I look back at the "last-minute decision" that was made to finish my first year of Charis while I was still living in Alabama, and I could see that the Lord truly knows what He is doing. He spoke to me during my forty-day fast to finish my first year, so I could begin my second year when I arrived in Colorado. It was no small feat to finish about three-fourths of my first year in about a four-to-five-month window, but I knew the Lord was asking me to do it. It was because of this and the financial miracle I received on 12/12/12 that I was able to stay at home with Daniel while Aaron finished his final year.

During Aaron's spring break, we traveled to Roanoke, Virginia, and visited, believing this was where the Lord was leading us to move after Bible college. We found a home in a historic area of Roanoke and made an offer. The offer was accepted, and we were overjoyed. Roanoke was only about two hours from Aaron's hometown, and it was in driving distance to my parents' home in the North Carolina Mountains. We both agreed that Roanoke would be a beautiful place to raise a family, and I was also ready for any sort of break from Colorado winters.

In May, Aaron graduated from Bible college, and in June, we packed up our condo and moved to Roanoke, Virginia. There were signs that something was not right all along the way, but Aaron and I chose to blindly ignore them. We did not intentionally oppose the Lord or knowingly resist the Holy Spirit, but looking back, I can now see clearly that we did just that ignorantly. Aaron missed the mountains of Virginia very much, and I missed the "south." We thought Roanoke was the perfect place, but there was a problem—all of our human reasoning and all our plans were not part of the Lord's plans, and we discovered this almost as soon as we moved.

From the moment we moved into our new home, it was as if we were being resisted on every side and every front. The resistance was severe, and the spiritual warfare was nonstop. We had little to no peace and were quite honestly miserable. We prayed, fasted, asked others to pray for us, made adjustments, did anything and everything we knew to do, and nothing changed. Our marriage was suffering, and it felt like we were at odds with each other all the time.

Despite all the adversity, I found out I was pregnant about a month after we arrived in Roanoke. It was a joy to be pregnant again, and I was full of hope. Daniel was a joy as well. He was crawling and curious and kept us constantly on our toes. Even with the difficulties, we could still find so much to be thankful for, and we were still hopeful and thankful. Aaron and Daniel came with me to see the new baby on the very first visit to the doctor. It was during that visit that we discovered there was no heartbeat. We were devastated to hear "I am so sorry" instead of "congratulations." I felt like someone had punched and sucked all the air out of me. I was numb head to toe when the doctor said we could do some more testing to see if there may be any chance of life. We did all the testing and found out from a medical point that the baby was gone. There was nothing more to be done.

I was sent home to wait for the baby to miscarry. I was told that since the pregnancy hormone levels were dropping, it would only be a matter of time. Aaron and I prayed and sought the Lord for wisdom and comfort. I was ready to believe the Lord to raise the dead since raising the dead is clearly demonstrated in the Bible. When Jesus sent out the twelve apostles in Matthew 10, He sent them out with specific instructions that included raising the dead.

> "Don't go to the Gentiles or the Samaritans, but only to the people of Israel—God's lost sheep. Go and announce to them that the Kingdom of Heaven is near. Heal the sick, raise the dead, cure those with leprosy, and cast out demons. Give as freely as you have received!"
>
> Matthew 10:5–8 (NLT)

As I prayed, the Comforter began to comfort. "But the Comforter, which is the Holy Ghost, whom the Father will send in my name, he shall teach you all things, and bring all things to your remembrance, whatsoever I have said unto you" (John 14:26, KJV). The Lord spoke a scripture to my heart that I knew quite well. "He who is least in the Kingdom of heaven is greater than he" (Matthew 11:11, NKJV). I knew the Lord was speaking to me from Matthew 11. It was a scripture and reference to John the Baptist. I looked up the entire scripture, read it, and began to weep.

"Assuredly, I say to you, among those born of women there has not risen one greater than John the Baptist; but he who is least in the Kingdom of heaven is greater than he. And from the days of John the Baptist until now the Kingdom of heaven suffers violence, and the violent take it by force."

Matthew 11:11–12 (NKJV)

I felt the Lord was telling me that our baby was now in heaven, and it was well. I believed with all my heart the Lord was showing me that because our baby was now in heaven and a part of the Kingdom of heaven, she/he was actually greater than any earthly leader—even a leader as great as John the Baptist. What was the bottom line? Even the least person in heaven has a perfected, immortal body while those of us on earth are still living in a fallen world. They are citizens of heaven, living in heaven. I began rejoicing as I could see and imagine our baby in heaven. Then the Lord gave me another scripture. I believed the Lord said, "...I will go to him one day, but he cannot return to me" (2 Samuel 12:23, NIV). I also found great comfort in this scripture. I believed the Lord was clearly saying that I would one day see this child again, but it would be in heaven, not on earth.

David had actually spoken this in 2 Samuel 12 when he lost his newborn baby, "David replied, 'I fasted and wept while the child was alive, for I said, "Perhaps the LORD will be gracious to me and let the child live." But why should I fast when he is dead? Can I bring him back again? I will go to him one day, but he cannot return to me'" (2 Samuel 12:22–23, NLT).

I made peace with it all that day. It did not mean that I understood it all, but I knew that God was good, and I knew He was speaking to me that it was well. I had a promise and a hope that I would one day meet our child in heaven, and for now, it was enough. I let the baby go and grieved the loss with the Lord and with Aaron. I knew the Lord would give us joy for our mourning (Isaiah 61:3).

> The Spirit of the Sovereign Lord is upon me, for the LORD has anointed me to bring good new to the poor. He has sent me to comfort the brokenhearted and to proclaim that captives will be released and prisoners will be freed. He has sent me to tell those who mourn that the time of the LORD's favor has come, and with it, the day of God's anger against their enemies. To all who mourn in Israel, he will give a crown of beauty for ashes, a joyous blessing instead of mourning, festive praise instead of despair. In their righteousness, they will be like great oaks that the LORD has planted for his own glory.

> Isaiah 61:1–3 (NLT)

About four months later, on December 20, 2016, I woke up at 4:30 a.m. and heard, "I have been instated to watch over you." I knew in that moment that it was an angel speaking to me, although I saw nothing. I only heard the single sentence that was spoken to me, but heaven had my attention. I had never before heard anything similar spoken to me, nor since. I knew this was significant, although I did not understand at the time exactly what was taking place.

According to Merriam-Webster, the definition of "instate" (verb) is "to set or establish in a rank or office: to install."

On January 31, 2017, I found out I was pregnant. We were overjoyed with the news and so thankful. This was about six weeks after I woke up hearing the angel speak to me. I believe the angel I heard speak to me was announcing his assignment and "office" to watch over me and to watch over the baby. I believe this angel knew that our baby was coming, and I believe he was there to watch over and protect every moment of that child's life from conception and even before.

This pregnancy was quite different and much easier than being pregnant with Daniel. I was sick some, but it was quite mild, and I felt great most of the time. I was also busy with Daniel, who was now an active toddler and full of endless energy. We all went together again to the first doctor's appointment to see the baby, and we got to hear a perfect, healthy, strong heartbeat. I cried very happy tears.

It was then early spring in Roanoke. We had been living in Roanoke for just about nine months, but it felt like years. They were very long and difficult months, and Aaron and I finally had "the talk." I will never forget it. We were sitting at our dining room table when I said what I had feared to speak for quite some time, "Aaron, do you think we are really supposed to be here?" We discussed all the difficulties, the warfare, but it was the lack of peace that was the real defining issue to me. The Bible clearly says the Lord will lead people with peace. Colossians 3:15 tells us to let the peace of God rule in our hearts. The original Greek word for "rule" in this scripture is actually the same word that is used for "govern." We are to let peace "govern" our decisions and rule telling us if we are "in" God's will or "out." We prayed together and asked the Lord to show us the truth.

In May, we found out we were having another boy. He was healthy and perfect, and we were so grateful. I was truly enjoying being pregnant, and I can honestly say I felt so beautiful. There was something so amazing about carrying life. I counted it one of the greatest privileges of my life to be a part of bringing forth a precious life into this world, not once but twice.

On October 2, 2017, David Joshua Butte was born. He weighed eight pounds and twelve ounces and was absolutely perfect. We had prayed for a healthy, full-term baby and both our boys were healthy, full-term babies. David was so beautiful, and he fully captured our hearts from the first moment we saw him and held him.

Our family of three was now four, and we entered into another time of great blessing and promise. David's first months at home were blessed and were similar to the special season we experienced in Colorado when we brought Daniel home. There were still difficulties and warfare, but there was a marked increase in the presence of God and in miracles, signs, and wonders. It was clear that the Lord's hand was on us, and His protection and promises were at work in our lives.

On multiple occasions, David was spared as a newborn from severe sickness when everyone else in the home was seriously ill. Aaron, myself, and Daniel were all fighting a stomach virus that proved to be so severe that I had to get prescription medication to stop throwing up, and Daniel did as well. We were violently ill, and I was gripped with fear for our precious newborn. We stood on the promises of God for divine protection and declared Psalm 91 over David. Despite me breastfeeding David and having constant close contact with him, he never got sick. He appeared to be immune. This was nothing short of a miracle.

Just a few weeks later, all three of us were sick again with a virus that was dreadful and fierce. The coughing and assault on the lungs and the entire respiratory system felt quite dangerous, and Daniel and I were both eventually put on antibiotics and steroids. Again, I cried out to the Lord for mercy for our newborn and stood on the Word of God for divine protection. Psalm 91 promises divine protection and angelic help:

When we live our lives within the shadow of God Most High, our secret hiding place, we will always be shielded from harm. How then could evil prevail against us or disease infect us? God sends angels with special orders to protect you wherever you go, defending you from all harm.

Psalm 91:9–11 (TPT)

I was lying in bed one night suffering from the sickness and gripped with fear for David. I was also praying. All of a sudden, the almost unbelievable occurred. I saw an angel step out from what I can only describe as the thin veil that separates heaven from earth. He looked at me as if to say, "I'm here, and nothing is going to happen to that baby." And then He went back into the veil and was gone.

I sat there motionless for some time, trying to process what had just taken place. I was so comforted by the experience, and I believed that it could have been the angel who first announced himself to me right before David was conceived. He said everything that needed to be said when he looked at me. Despite all the care and close contact a newborn baby requires, David never even had a sniffle. Again, he appeared to be immune.

As David's first Christmas approached, we celebrated as a family the goodness and faithfulness of our great God. He truly preserves us from trouble. I can't help but think of Psalm 66.

"Praise God, all you peoples. Praise him everywhere and let everyone know you love him! There's no doubt about it: God holds our lives safely in his hands. He's the one who keeps us faithfully following him" (Psalm 66:8–9, TPT).

Please pray with me.

161

Father, thank You for holding us safely in Your hands (Psalm 66:9). We will remember the great things You have done for us and celebrate them, for You alone are God, and there is no other (Isaiah 46:9). "You make Your messengers into winds of the Spirit, and all Your ministers become flames of fire" (Psalm 104:4, TPT). Send Your fire, Lord! We want to burn for You. Set us ablaze and send us out. Lord, use us to bring the good news to the poor, proclaim liberty to the captives, restore sight to the blind, set the oppressed free, and announce that the time of Your favor has come (Luke 4:18–19). It has indeed come, and we want to be a part of bringing in Your great end-time harvest. Father, we repent of any way that we have partnered with the spirit of death that has invaded our culture and way of life. We repent for the spiritual blindness that covers so much of America—as well as much of the world—and sadly has crept into the church. Father, forgive us and give us eyes to see and ears to hear the truth (Proverbs 20:12). Somehow this spiritual blindness has covered the eyes and callused the hearts of so many that we as a nation would accept the brutal, violent, and inhumane murder of the most innocent among us—the unborn. This should not be! A mother's womb should be the most safe and protected place on the planet, and yet today, it is the most dangerous. Today it is the only place that it is legal to kill a human. This is an abomination. This is the greatest injustice of our lifetime, and one day, future generations will look back on this with great disapproval. If you have had an abortion or been an advocate for abortion, you can ask the Lord to forgive you today and be set free. He will absolutely forgive you, cleanse you, and heal you from the pain of abortion. Today can be your day to step up and out of darkness. Father, we know that abortion kills the baby and wounds the mother, but we also know that You can heal any wound and set any captive free. Lord, we pray for each and every person reading this to be flooded with the absolute truth of Your Word. We pray for conviction, for godly sorrow that leads to repentance (2 Corinthians 7:10), and for every lie to be exposed for what is. Jeremiah 1:5 (NLT) says, "I knew you before I formed you in your mother's womb. Before you were born I set you apart and appointed you as my prophet to the nations." We repent for the murder of hundreds of millions of innocent babies, and Father, we ask You to have mercy on us. We also pray for anyone reading this who has been a proponent of abortion or has had an abortion. We pray for their hearts to be turned to the truth and for them to find true peace in You. There is no condemnation to those of us in Christ Jesus (Romans 8:1), and who the Son sets free is free indeed (John 8:36). In Jesus' mighty name, we pray. Amen.

Chapter 17: Divine Realignment

The summer before David was born, we took a family vacation to Sandbridge Beach, Virginia. Although Sandbridge is technically part of Virginia Beach, it is about fifteen miles away from the resort area of Virginia Beach and is considered to be more of a secluded beach area and a hideaway. We were looking for just that in a vacation, and Sandbridge did not disappoint. I was six months pregnant with David at the time, and Daniel was almost two. We fell in love with Sandbridge and found its gorgeous beaches to be the escape we had been longing for and needing.

It was on this week-long trip to Sandbridge that the Lord clearly spoke to Aaron and me about Roanoke, our missteps, and repositioning ourselves for divine alignment. It felt almost from the first minute we arrived on our vacation that we were able to relax and take a deep breath for the first time in a long time. It felt like we left the nonstop spiritual warfare in Roanoke, and we were able to enjoy a few days, having real peace and joy again. We had prayed at our dining room table for the Lord to please tell us what we were supposed to do, and if we were not supposed to be in Roanoke, we were willing to make whatever adjustments that might require.

My daily routine always includes morning prayer, but with toddlers and newborns, that was more difficult. I still did my best to make it a priority, and while on vacation, I fully enjoyed praying and watching the sun come up over the Atlantic every morning. There was no doubt that something different was happening as I was hearing the Lord speak to me so clearly, and finally getting clarity and wisdom about our family and our situation in Roanoke. I was praying every morning in Roanoke as well, but there it felt like the heavens were brass. At Sandbridge, we were experiencing a sort of breakthrough.

Aaron was experiencing the same thing, and we were both hearing the same thing from the Lord. We felt He was showing us that Roanoke was "our idea" and not His. We essentially made our own plan and then asked the Lord to bless it. The Bible says not to despise it when the Lord disciplines you (Proverbs 3:11), and we were coming to terms with His discipline. We felt He was telling us that He had a much better plan for our family than we had for ourselves, and we were being asked to trust in His plan and not our own.

> My child, when the Lord God speaks to you, never take his words lightly, and never be upset when he corrects you. For the Father's discipline comes only from his passionate love and pleasure for you. Even when it seems like his correction is harsh, it's still better than any father on earth gives to his child.

> Proverbs 3:11–12 (TPT)

On our vacation, we asked the Lord to forgive us for doing our own thing and repented of the mess we had made in the process. We repented from our hearts and made the commitment to the Lord to move wherever He wanted to send us and do whatever He wanted us to do. We knew this would not be an overnight fix as I was six months pregnant and did not feel He wanted to uproot us right as David was about to be born. We also had a home we had purchased just a year earlier and wondered how the Lord would work it all out, but we trusted Him. We were willing to do anything to find true peace and the center of His perfect will again.

We did not want to leave Sandbridge, and the drive home was sad and long. We had enjoyed the serenity we found there and did not want to go back to the battle zone we had come to expect in

Roanoke, but we came back surrendered, and that shifted much. Yes, we still had battles there, but things were different when we returned. We now knew we would be moving, and we had a precious baby to look forward to meeting soon. The months spent waiting for David were better, and we were seriously praying and seeking what the Lord would have us to do. We even prayed about moving across the country for Aaron to go back to school at a ministry located in California. We seriously thought the Lord might be asking us to do that, and although it would be difficult, we did commit to go if that was His leading. However, in time we felt while it might have been a good idea, it was not a God-idea and took moving cross-country off the table.

David was born in October, and shortly after his birth, we received a request from an international ministry we had been partners with for some time. I had been partners with this ministry since I was single and watched their broadcast daily. I found it to be a tremendous blessing and was proud to sow into what they were doing all over the world. The letter was asking us to sow a $2,000 seed, and to be honest, I did not have the desire to give that kind of money with a new baby and the costs we were facing as parents, but I could not throw the letter away. I put it on our kitchen shelf where I could see it and continued to pray.

We were partners with this ministry, but we were not giving that kind of money to them. In fact, that would be the largest seed we would have ever sown into their ministry, by far, if we were to give what they were asking. We received the request in early fall, and it was a Thanksgiving offering. The head of the ministry was asking us to give a one-time offering for Thanksgiving. I kept praying about it but was having a hard time actually committing to give that amount, but I could not throw the letter away. Finally, months later and weeks after Thanksgiving had come and gone, I heard the Lord speak to me as I walked through the kitchen and passed by the letter on the shelf. "I am not trying to get something from you. I am trying to get something to you," I heard. I stopped on a dime. It was the Lord. He was speaking. I heard again, "I am not trying to get something from you. I am trying to get something to you." I looked up and saw the envelope from the ministry.

When Aaron got home from work, I told him what happened, and we agreed to give the $2,000 immediately. I wrote the check that night, and when I tried to put the check in a different envelope from the original "Thanksgiving" one, I felt the Holy Spirit resist me. I felt the Lord was telling me He wanted me to send it in the original request that was for Thanksgiving. It had gold writing on it and was quite beautiful. Despite it being long past Thanksgiving, I did as I felt the Lord was leading me. I felt He was being very specific, and I was learning to "lean not to my own understanding" and do as He leads—even if it doesn't make sense. We sent in our seed and believed for a hundred-fold harvest (Genesis 26:12).

A few months later, a large envelope arrived in the mail, and before I could even open it, I could see it was an invitation. As I looked on the return address, I saw it was from the large ministry we had sown into some time earlier. Upon opening the invitation, I found a "save the date" card for an upcoming partner weekend scheduled for the spring in Virginia Beach, Virginia. The card had a few details like the time, dates, where, and when, but what I found the most encouraging was the theme of the weekend—"A Time of Refreshing." I was excited, encouraged, and curious about this partner weekend we were being invited to, but most of all, I wondered why we had been invited. Yes, we had been partners with this ministry for years, but we were not large donors at that time. The $2,000 we sowed was by far the largest seed we had ever sown into this ministry.

When the full invitation arrived in the mail, I discovered that we were being invited to a full weekend getaway complete with worship, teaching, and personal ministry time. All of our accommodations and food were included. We just needed to RSVP and get ourselves there. Since we were just a five-hour drive from Virginia Beach, it would not be difficult. We had been praying about it ever since we first heard about the event, and I wanted to go, but we would need the Lord to work out the details. David was just a few months old, and Daniel was two. We had never left both of them with anyone overnight. The idea of being away with my husband for even just two nights alone was something we would have loved to hope for but would honestly say probably wasn't possible. We were also very particular about leaving them with anyone. We had one babysitter at that time, and she was the children's minister at our church and studying to be a NICU nurse. We absolutely trusted her but felt she would need help for a full weekend. So we prayed, and the Lord worked it out where another young girl from our church that we knew and trusted would stay with the boys as well. We felt comfortable with both the girls staying with them for the weekend and felt the Lord was leading us to go to Virginia Beach. We confirmed that we would be coming and began looking forward to April.

When the weekend arrived, we went expecting. We were not sure what we were expecting, but we were full of expectancy. We were not disappointed. We met many other believers and enjoyed their fellowship; we met many people we had seen on television for years and were blessed by actually being about to speak with them in person, and we were enormously touched by seeing the fruit of what this ministry was doing in America and all over the world. I found myself crying over and over again seeing the hands and feet of Jesus at work on planet earth. I was being powerfully touched by the Lord and was experiencing His peace and joy. We were asking the Lord to send us and use us, but it was clear that we would have to leave Roanoke to find, follow, and fulfill His perfect plan for our lives. Could it be that He had directed us to this weekend to show us where He wanted to use us next? I wasn't sure at the time, but it was certainly something Aaron and I would pray through together. Hope was springing to life right in front of my very eyes, and it was producing great excitement.

On the final day of the weekend, we went to a Sunday morning communion service. After a weekend of seeing what this ministry was doing all over the world, I had been moved time and time again; and yes, I had been greatly convicted. I was a mother of two very small children, and they needed me, but I wanted to serve more, give more, and do more for Christ and His cause. Over the weekend, I had even been invited to travel on an upcoming missions trip that ministers to orphans and widows across the globe. My heart leaped for joy at the invitation, but then I realized that it would be virtually impossible for me with the boys. I had to decline. The one thing I knew we could do was give. Even if we could not go, I knew we could give money to help others and send others who could go. I knew the Lord was leading us to sow another seed into this ministry, and we wanted it to be a generous seed.

One of the most quoted scriptures in the Bible would have to be "...God loves a cheerful giver" (2 Corinthians 9:7, NIV). In the past, I have to admit I have sown financial seeds and not been cheerful about it, but I was cheerful about this seed. Aaron and I both were cheerful and expectant. We did not understand exactly what the Lord was doing, but we were willing to be obedient and trust Him.

Let giving flow from your heart, not from a sense of religious duty. Let it spring up freely from the joy of giving—all because God loves hilarious generosity! Yes, God is more than ready to overwhelm you with every form of grace, so that you will have more than enough of everything—every moment and in every way. He will make you overflow with abundance in every good thing you do. Just as the Scriptures say about the one who trusts in him: Because he has sown extravagantly and given to the poor, his kindness and generous deeds will never be forgotten.

2 Corinthians 9:7–9 (TPT)

At the communion service, Aaron and I went forward together and sowed a $5,000 seed. Although this was not the largest seed we had ever sown, it was the largest seed we had ever sown into this ministry. I learned almost immediately after my conversion the blessing of being a faithful tither and giver. I had been tithing and giving my entire born-again life, and Aaron grew up doing the same. We both believed in it and knew the blessing found it. As we walked up together, sowing this seed, we were also sowing in expectancy. We prayed over it and believed the Lord would multiply it. We specifically prayed for a hundred-fold harvest according to Genesis 26:12.

"Then Isaac sowed in that land, and reaped in the same year a hundredfold; and the LORD blessed him. The man began to prosper, and continued prospering until he became very prosperous" (Genesis 26:12–13, NKJV).

When the weekend was over and it was time to go, we packed our bags, and I cried as we left. They were sad tears. I did not want to go. I wanted to see my sweet boys, but I wanted to stay in His presence. Nothing satisfies like the sweet presence of God. It had been a weekend full of the presence of God, and that was very hard to leave.

We were also starting to put some pieces of the puzzle together. Our vacation in Sandbridge, where we experienced breakthrough and great peace, wasn't far from where we had been staying and visiting for the spring partner weekend. They were both technically in Virginia Beach. Coincidence? *Maybe*, I thought, *but maybe not*. On the drive home, Aaron and I prayed from the depths of our hearts and asked the Lord to speak clearly to us what He was saying, and we asked Him to make it plain. In my heart, I already knew the answer. As we were sowing our $5,000 seed that morning, I heard the Lord whisper to my heart, "Sow where you want to go."

The joy of seeing our two little boys as we walked into our home in Roanoke was wonderful. We were back, but it felt like a part of us was already in Virginia Beach. It was early April, and by May, we felt we had the Lord's confirmation on what we already knew in our hearts. We felt the Lord was leading us to Virginia Beach. We put our home on the market, prayed for it to sell quickly, and believed to get the full asking price.

We had five serious offers the first week, and we were overjoyed! It looked like we would be in Virginia Beach by the summer, but to our utter unbelief, all five offers fell through. I believe many factors played into this, including spiritual warfare, but God's Word will not return void (Isaiah 55:11). His Word promises that what the enemy intends for evil, the Lord will work out for our good (Genesis 50:20). It was clear that we had an adversary fighting us, and we knew if we were going to move, we would have to fight that battle in His strength. We also knew we would not win the battle by "wishing and hoping" things would just "work out." We were in a real battle, and we would need to partner with the Lord and hear from heaven to get His strategies and perspective on things.

We continued showing the home through the month of May, but we had no other offers. In early June, we prepared to go back to Virginia Beach for another family vacation in Sandbridge. We had booked this vacation in early winter without knowing the events that would unfold in the spring. The vacation seemed providential from the start. It was a joy to be back in Virginia Beach. Sandbridge was amazing, and it was truly a delight to be there as a family. Just a year prior, I had been pregnant with David; now, we were enjoying the beach with David and Daniel.

While we were on this trip, I received a phone call from the ministry we had sowed into months earlier. A woman whom I had never spoken to left a message on my phone requesting me to call her back. Curious, I called her. She worked for the television show associated with this ministry and asked if I would speak with her about my testimony. She said she had been told that I attended the most recent partner weekend and that she had been told I had "a powerful testimony." I was honestly baffled as I did not remember sharing my testimony with anyone that weekend, but I was greatly honored that they had interest in hearing about my story of coming to faith. She asked if I would have any objections or interest in having my testimony air on the show. I told her I would be honored. We set a time and date to discuss my testimony further and to see if my story would be a good fit for the program. Before I hung up, I had seen her phone number on my caller id and knew she was in Virginia Beach. I could not help but share the irony of the situation since she was calling me from Virginia Beach, and I was in Virginia Beach on vacation. It all seemed very serendipitous. It was beginning to look like things were aligning for us in Virginia Beach.

On July 20, 2018, less than four months after we sowed the $5,000 dollar seed in Virginia Beach, I received a phone call that was part of the breakthrough we were praying and waiting to receive. I was being gifted a portion of my inheritance that totaled $500,000 cash. Yes, it was exactly a hundred-time harvest—to the penny—on the $5,000 dollar seed we had sowed just a few months earlier.

After we tithed on the harvest, we used a portion to pay off the mortgage on our home in Roanoke. Yes, we knew we were moving, but it was our heart's desire to be totally debt-free, and we wanted our debt-free life to begin immediately. Becoming totally debt-free was wonderful, and we saw an immediate breakthrough in the atmosphere of our home as well as increased peace and joy in our home and family after we became the outright owners of our home rather than our bank.

It was also around this time that I spoke in great detail with the woman from the television ministry about my testimony. After hearing most of my story, she said she felt my testimony would be a good fit for the show and asked if I was comfortable with progressing to the next steps in the process. I said I was, and we set a date for a team to come to our home and tape my testimony as well as footage of our family. In mid-August, the crew came and filmed for the better part of a day, and we were told to wait for a future air date to be set sometime soon.

On October 3, 2018, my testimony aired, and it was an incredible experience to watch myself on the television program I had made such a huge part of my daily life. I watched this show almost every day for years, and it was always such an enormous blessing to me. Now I was hoping that my story was a blessing to someone else needing hope and encouragement.

I remember watching this show as an addict. I was in full-blown addiction to prescription pills and alcohol and flipping through the channels when I remember stopping to hear what they had to say because there was something different about the show. Now it seemed as if my life had come full circle. My life was being used to minister to others. It was enormously humbling, and I could not watch my testimony without crying. I cried over and over again at the goodness of our great God! He did not have to save my life, but He did. He did not have to go to the cross, but He did. He lives, and today I live because He lives.

Despite all the wonderful things that were unfolding and the blessings that were being unpacked in our lives, we were still ready and waiting to move. We prayed, fasted, sowed, and did anything and everything we could to try to get our home to sell. We had interest but no offers. When our realtor's six-month contract was up, we began looking into finding a new agent. Our home was in one of the most sought-after and desirable areas in Roanoke, and the home was beautiful. There was really no reason why the home had not sold, and in all honesty, it should and would have sold the first week. But we know God works all things together for the good of those who love Him and are called according to His purpose (Romans 8:28).

In November, we hired a new realtor. She was arguably the best in Roanoke, and we felt the Lord led us straight to her. By Thanksgiving, we had an offer, and it was accepted. I could not help but remember the great lengths the Lord went to speak to me about sowing that "Thanksgiving seed" one year earlier. What a year it had been, and everything good that came in that year seemed to almost directly or indirectly be tied to that first "Thanksgiving seed." That Thanksgiving, we celebrated greatly, and we were so thankful for our home being "under contract." Now we could begin the process of starting our new lives in Virginia Beach. I'm really glad we sowed that seed. Obedience surely brings blessing. The Lord used that seed to change our lives.

In December, we found a new home in Virginia Beach, not far from Sandbridge. We just knew it was our home and made an offer. Despite multiple offers, our offer was accepted. Because we had the financial miracle that took place in July, we were also able to pay cash for the home. We got a great deal on it as it appraised for over $110,000 more than what we paid. It was also the 2018 St. Jude's Dream Home, so the home had a great deal of PR and publicity. We did not know any of this when we first found it, but we enjoyed having a somewhat renowned home.

As part of the St. Jude Dream Home Giveaway, St. Jude sells tickets at $100 apiece, and the winner wins a brand-new home.[5] We purchased our home from the man who won it, and since no one had ever lived in it previously, it was purchased as a "new construction." We saw the Lord's hand of favor in it all. Our beloved Sandbridge was just a five-minute drive from our front door, and our local grocery store was the same store we shopped at on vacation. We joked and enjoyed living where we used to vacation.

We moved to Virginia Beach in faith. Aaron did not have a job when we moved, and I still felt the Lord was leading me to be home with the boys full time. So we continued to pray and believed the Lord would lead Aaron to the job He had prepared for him. Despite applying for multiple positions at the ministry headquartered in Virginia Beach, Aaron heard nothing back. For weeks it appeared to be a closed door of opportunity, and Aaron had to begin looking for work elsewhere. He found a job working in sales for a Christian company, but he was, in all honesty, miserable. He worked there for several months when the unexpected happened.

Someone from the ministry we partnered with reached out to Aaron concerning his past applications for employment. They had

5   St. Jude Children's Research Hospital, stjude.org.

an opening in a department that Aaron had not considered nor applied for but asked if he would be interested in applying for the job. Aaron's first instinct was no. It was a job that required a background in construction, and Aaron had worked multiple different jobs in construction and carpentry while in Roanoke and was miserable at them all. He said he never wanted to work in any sort of construction ever again. Well, never say never. After much prayer and leaning in to hear the Lord's heart, Aaron changed his mind and applied for the job. He interviewed and was able to see exactly what he would be doing and felt very different after meeting the team he would be working with. He was offered the job and started almost immediately. He would be a part of the team that designed, built, and constructed all the sets for the television and broadcasting arm of the ministry. The Lord wastes nothing. Those years in Roanoke where Aaron was so unhappy working various jobs were not wasted years. Now the Lord was using what he learned during those years and letting it be used for His glory and divine design. Aaron loved his job from day one, and we celebrated what the Lord had done.

It felt like the Lord had parted the Red Sea for us, and we had crossed over on dry ground. Aaron was as happy and content as I had ever seen him, and our family was loving our new life in Virginia Beach. We were grateful, and life looked to be so full of promise for us. We enjoyed our first summer as a family in our new home and took full advantage of living at the beach. We did not know at the time that the world would look so different in only about six months. Like many families, our family was challenged by the coronavirus pandemic, but we knew the Lord wastes nothing, and we are told to rejoice in all circumstances (1 Thessalonians 5:16–18).

What took place in our lives during the pandemic was wonderful and miraculous. As we drew near to God, He drew near to us (James

4:8). The pandemic was life-changing, and both Aaron and I found ourselves in a much more intimate and devoted relationship with the Lord than ever before. The enemy wanted to use the pandemic to destroy us, but the Lord used it to draw us closer to Him.

"Let joy be your continual feast. Make your life a prayer. And in the midst of everything be always giving thanks, for this is God's perfect plan for you in Christ Jesus" (1 Thessalonians 5:16–18, TPT).

Please pray with me.

Father, thank You that You waste nothing. Even our trials and temptations can be turned around for good and used to bring You glory. We thank You that Jesus bore the entirety of the curse on the cross that we could and would walk in the blessing. He was cursed so we could be blessed (Galatians 3:13–14). Thank You, Jesus. We speak the blessing over our lives and the lives of our children and our children's children right now. "May the LORD bless you and protect you. May the LORD smile on you and be gracious to you. May the LORD show you his favor and give you his peace" (Numbers 6:24–26, NLT). We speak shalom— peace—over our lives and the lives of our families. We thank You for divine order in our lives and the lives of our families. We take authority over chaos and the fog of confusion that would cripple or defeat Your people. We say no to the enemy's counterfeit plans that would bankrupt, cripple, and/or defeat Your children. Thank You for divine realignments, divine assignments, and the revealing of divine purpose and destiny. We believe by faith that today is the day of salvation (2 Corinthians 6:2) and that Your perfect will is coming to pass in our lives right now. In Jesus' mighty name, we pray. Amen!

Chapter 18: An Appeal to Heaven

We had been in our new home in Virginia Beach for just over a year when the pandemic began in 2020. Like many families, our entire lives were disrupted during the first few months of quarantine and lockdowns. We experienced many ups and downs during that time, but we found the Lord to be true to His Word and always faithful.

On April 21, 2020, the Lord called Aaron and me to a forty-day fast. This was the first forty-day fast I had been called to complete since being married or with children. This was also the first forty-day fast Aaron and I would complete together. The fast started shortly after Easter and would end on Pentecost Sunday. I knew if the Lord was calling us to this kind of fast, He had big things in the works, and that would also mean the enemy would be doing all he could to steal, kill, and destroy in the process. We knew in our hearts we were entering a *kairos* season. *Kairos* is an ancient Greek word found in the scriptures. According to Merriam-Webster, *kairos* is defined as "a time when conditions are right for the accomplishment of a crucial action or an opportune and decisive moment." Indeed, we felt the weight of it all. We knew the Lord was about to shift things.

Almost a year earlier, Aaron and I began a new journey with the Lord that was taking us into uncharted waters. Both of us have always been patriotic, but it felt like the Lord was birthing in us a deep and passionate love for our country and the Christian foundation America was established upon. We began devouring documentaries on the birth of our nation, our founding fathers, their Christian faith, and almost anything tied to the Revolutionary War and the colonial period. We began to really unpack and digest what took place during the American Revolution and began to deeply admire the patriots who took on tyranny and fought so bravely so that this county would be born. We saw the hand of God in almost every story we read, movie we watched, and piece of history we learned. It was around this time that we first learned about the flag named "An Appeal to Heaven."

In the fall of 1775, a fleet of six ships known as "Washington's Cruisers" was constructed by the colonists. The vessels were sent out to capture British ammunition, arms, and provisions headed to the British Army in the Colonies. These six cruisers flew the very first national flag known as "An Appeal to Heaven Flag" or "The Pinetree Flag." It was a white flag with a green pine tree and the motto "An Appeal to Heaven."[6]

> Thus, when the early militiamen and naval officers flew the Pinetree Flag emblazoned with its motion "An Appeal for Heaven," it was not some random act with little significance or meaning. Instead, they sought to march into battle with a recognition of God's Providence and their reliance on the King of Kings to right the wrongs which they had suffered. The Pinetree Flag represents a vital part of America's history and an important step on the journey to reaching a national flag during the early days of the War for Independence.[7]

Aaron and I learned about this flag, and something about it began to burn deeply in our hearts. I found a man in New England who recreated Revolution-era flags and hand-painted them to create beautiful signboards. They were exceptional, and I commissioned

6   "An Appeal to Heaven Flag," USAFlagCo, www.usaflagco.com/products/pine-tree-flag.
7   "An Appeal to Heaven Flag," WallBuilders, last modified September 2020, http://www.wallbuilders.com/an-appeal-to-heaven-flag/.

him to create an "An Appeal to Heaven" signboard for Aaron's Christmas gift in 2019. I planned on putting it in the center of our home. The artist was delayed, and Aaron's Christmas gift was delayed as well. Then the pandemic began, and it was delayed again. The artist was apologetic and offered to give us our money back. We told him that we still wanted the signboard, and he agreed to get it to us as soon as possible. Aaron received it at the end of our forty-day fast. It was months late, but it felt like it came right on time. The "An Appeal to Heaven" signboard that hangs in the center of our home today has become our battle cry. We had no idea what our country would face in the upcoming months and how this flag would become the centerpiece of a national prayer movement, but the Lord knew. He put it in our hearts then, and when facing tyranny today, we can "appeal to heaven" just like they did almost 250 years ago.

The book you are reading today was something the Lord put in my heart to write shortly after my conversion. I always knew I would write this book. I did not know when or exactly what would be in it, but I knew I would write a book(s) for the Lord. He spoke it to me, and it was prophesied over me many times. About ten years ago, while living in Fairhope, Alabama, I sat down and started to write a book. I wrote two full chapters before the Lord clearly told me that it was not time. I threw the chapters away and waited for the Lord. Almost every year or every few years, I would get such a strong urge and desire to write that I would pray and seek the Lord, and yet I never felt released to move forward. During our forty-day fast, that happened again, but this time it was by far the strongest and deepest desire I had ever experienced. I was ready to write. I wanted to write, and I just knew the Lord wanted me to start. However, the Lord spoke to me during the fast, and instead of releasing me to write, He gave me an instruction. He told me to begin a mentorship under an apostolic female minister based out of Arizona. Although this was not on my "radar," I respected this woman deeply and admired her ministry and call. I quickly obeyed what I felt the Lord was telling me to do and began her mentorship immediately.

It was also around this time that we broke our forty-day fast on Pentecost Sunday 2020. Our church reopened its doors for a special Pentecost Worship service after being closed for months during the lockdown. Our family was there with bells on. It was good to be back in the house of the Lord. I can't help but think of what David said in Psalm 27:

> The one thing I ask of the LORD—the thing I seek most—is to live in the house of the LORD all the days of my life, delighting in the LORD's perfections and meditating in his Temple. For he will conceal me there when troubles come; he will hide me in his sanctuary. He will place me out of reach on a high rock. Then I will hold my head high above my enemies who surround me. I will offer sacrifices with shouts of joy, singing and praising the LORD with music.
>
> Psalm 27:4–6 (NLT)

Our church was back open. We were so grateful. Those months in lockdown were difficult, but not being in church was probably the hardest part of it all. The Bible says to not forsake the assembling of ourselves together (Hebrews 10:25). It's a warning and an admonition, and it should not be ignored even if there is a pandemic taking place. I love the way the Passion Translation says it, "This is not the time to pull away and neglect meeting together, as some have formed the habit of doing. In fact, we should come together even more frequently, eager to encourage and urge each other onward as we anticipate that day dawning" (Hebrews 10:25, TPT).

We broke our fast, we ate a big meal, and we celebrated Pentecost Sunday in church with our family and our family of fellow believers. We also took our boys to the beach, and I thought I would enjoy the time as much as possible, but something was wrong. I had no peace. Sitting right there on the beach, I began to pray. I spoke with the Lord candidly. I said, "Lord, we just finished a forty-day fast, and if there is any time I should be having peace, it's right now on this beautiful beach." I was watching our precious boys play, sitting next to my handsome husband and looking out over the Atlantic. "Why in the world would I not have peace?" I asked the Lord.

The next thing I saw was our home. I saw it in my mind's eye— my imagination—but I knew the Lord was speaking to me about it. We had experienced an onslaught of enormous spiritual warfare in our home and neighborhood during the months of the lockdown and pandemic. Then it was like the "lights went on." I saw and knew what the Lord was saying to me in an instant. The Lord wanted us to sell our home. This was the "dream home" we thought we always wanted, and to be honest, we had not even lived in it a year and a half. I sat there for a minute processing it all, and then I spoke out loud to the Lord. "So do You want us to sell it, Lord?" In that moment, peace flooded me like a river. I can tell you that this was tangible peace, and in scripture, it says that His peace flows like a river (Isaiah 66:12). Well, it was flowing to me in that moment like a river. The Lord answered my question with His peace. I had His answer.

For thus says the LORD: "Behold, I will extend peace to her like a river, And the glory of the Gentiles like a flowing stream. Then you shall feed; On her sides shall you be carried, And be dandled on her knees. As one whom his mother comforts, So I will comfort you; And you shall be comforted in Jerusalem."

Isaiah 66:12–13 (NKJV)

I sat there enjoying His peace and His presence right there on that beach. It was wonderful; the sun was shining, and my memories took me back to the same beach almost three years earlier to the day. I was pregnant with David, and our family was on vacation when the Lord spoke so clearly to us about our home in Roanoke. It felt like we were almost under an open heaven then, and in that moment, it felt like I was under an open heaven again. The Lord was speaking, and I was listening. I said, "Yes, Lord. We will sell the home, but You are going to have to tell Aaron." I was not about to tell him. This was the Lord's idea and His doing, so He would have to tell Aaron. I sat back and gave it to the Lord and enjoyed the moment. His peace is priceless.

At the end of the day, when both the boys were in bed, and we could take a deep breath and relax, we found ourselves standing in our kitchen together. Aaron looked over at me and told me that, earlier that day, he had started thinking about selling our home. I almost could not believe what I was hearing. I told him the Lord had shown me the exact same thing at the beach that day. Furthermore, I explained to him what I said to the Lord. I said, "You are going to have to tell Aaron." We were both relieved, and we laughed together. It was good to laugh. The enemy wanted to steal our joy through adverse circumstances, but the joy of the Lord will always be our strength (Nehemiah 8:10). We prayed together in the kitchen that night and told the Lord we would sell our home, and we asked Him to give us wisdom, discernment, and direction. We did not know how it would all work out, but we knew we were hearing His voice, and there was real excitement in both of us. We know we are not called to be "comfortable"; we are called to be obedient. We wanted to be obedient.

After more prayer, we began to step out into what we felt the Lord was leading us to do. It was early June, and it took several weeks to find the right realtor, but in the end, we found a Christian realtor who was among the best in the area. We shared our dreams for a new home with her, our testimonies of the Lord's faithfulness, and we shared the same faith. We knew she was the one. We put our home on the market on July 3, 2020. I felt like the Lord had asked me to not look at the homes on the market or what would be available to buy until it was time. He told me, "No peeking." It was as if He had a surprise and a great gift waiting for us. He also told me it was "extravagant."

That's all I knew from the Lord about our new home. Then he gave me a scripture that had a few more clues, "I have promised to rescue you from your oppression in Egypt. I will lead you to a land flowing with milk and honey..." (Exodus 3:17, NLT). The Lord was speaking that He was leading us to a "promised land." It sounded wonderful.

After our home was on the market, our realtor suggested we begin to look at new homes. It felt like we had just been through this process, and I did not even want to look. I asked her to send the homes she felt would be a good fit for our family. She sent us a lot of homes all over the area, and nothing she sent looked like what I felt the Lord was leading us to find and/or was the "gift" He wanted to give us. Our home at the time was located on a major road, and we were one of six homes located on a double cul-de-sac. We knew we wanted more privacy and more space for our family. We also knew it would be difficult to find a home as nice as the one we owned in our budget. But we knew it was also not impossible with the Lord.

All of the homes our realtor sent us were beautiful, nice, and most had more privacy and room, but none looked like the "extravagant" gift I felt the Lord was speaking that He wanted to give us. Aaron and I prayed again, and we got online and began to search for ourselves. We did a basic search in and around our budget, and almost at the very top of the list was what appeared to be a beautifully restored colonial home located in a rural area not far from where we lived at that time. It looked to be historic; it was grand, and yes, it was extravagant. It was a bit out of our budget but not impossible to bridge the gap. My heart raced because I knew it was our home. We jumped in the car as a family and drove to the home. It was only about ten minutes from our home at the time. When we drove up, my heart leaped with excitement. All my life, I had wanted to own a home like this. I had dreamed as a little girl of owning a grand, southern home. In Georgia, we had renowned antebellum mansions. This was Virginia, and while it wasn't antebellum, it was distinctly colonial and very Virginian, complete with magnolias and a forty-acre farm around it. I was utterly blown away. The boys played in the large yard, and we walked around and tried to see whatever we could see without being inside. I felt it was already ours.

Our realtor made an appointment with the listing agent for us to see the home as soon as possible. I cried at the showing, looking out the kitchen window over stunning fields full of corn. It was as if I had seen that view so many times before, and yet it was only my first time. I knew in my heart it would be a view I would look at in the future almost every day. We made an offer, and after several days of negotiations, we came to an agreement that was accepted by all parties. We would swap homes. Yes, there were a lot of details in the "swapping," but that is exactly what happened. The owner of the home we wanted to buy offered to buy the home that we wanted to sell as part of the deal. We were getting the home we wanted, and we were also selling the home we wanted to sell. We moved into our new home on August 7, 2020—just a few days over a month after putting our home on the market. It was a great miracle, and we were sincerely grateful.

There were so many moving parts to this miracle. We purchased the home for over $400 thousand dollars less than its original listing price. We paid cash for the home, and our offer was a cash offer, but when negotiations started to stall, both the listing agent and our realtor took reduced commissions to bridge the gap. We paid a fair price for the home, but it was also a good deal for all parties involved.

I had not lived out in the country since I lived at the farm, but I truly missed the quiet and peaceful life found in country living. Now, I would get to do it all over again with my family. Aaron grew up in a rural area, so this was in his heart as well. We were so thankful, and the boys seemed to come to new life in our new home too. All the extra space seemed to also be exactly what they needed. It was another new beginning for our family. It wasn't something we saw coming, but we were so glad the Lord had it in His heart for us. Now, we couldn't imagine it any other way.

In the fall of our first year in our new home, we took many trips to Colonial Williamsburg, taking in more of our history and sharing that history with our boys. Seeing Colonial Williamsburg brought history to new life for them and for us. We also could not help but appreciate our own colonial home even more as we visited Colonial Williamsburg and saw so many homes that looked so similar to ours. Was it a coincidence that the Lord had started this deep work in Aaron and myself that involved Colonial America's true history and our Christian roots and then proceeded to give us this colonial home? I don't think so, but as I reflect on it, I am reminded of one of my favorite verses from Proverbs, "It is the glory of God to conceal a matter, But the glory of kings is to search out a matter" (Proverbs 25:2, NKJV).

We intended to search out the matter with the Lord, and we continued visiting Williamsburg and Yorktown with our boys through the fall and winter months and even into the spring. The surrender and end of the Revolutionary War took place in Yorktown in 1781. There is a great monument in Yorktown overlooking the James River and commemorating the decisive victory that took place there. That victory secured the birth of the United States of America. On that exact spot, we prayed with our sons for our country. We prayed that the breakthrough and the miracles that took place for our great nation to be born would take place again and that the soul of America would turn back to God. We believe that the Lord sent us there to pray that day, and we believe our prayers were heard and that they will be answered. We believe America shall be saved.

I have often heard that sometimes things have to get worse before they get better. Watching what has looked like the downfall of America at the hands of corrupt politicians, dishonest political parties, and unprincipled journalists has definitively taken things from bad to worse and driven us only more to our knees in prayer. We watched in absolute disbelief as a fraudulent election took place, and an illegitimate man took the oath of president. We believe a majority of people know that the election was stolen but that a minority of dishonest individuals are controlling the narrative. It is, in fact, a false narrative—a lie. This minority is using their influence in media, social media, and various other platforms as well as politics and government to control and intentionally mislead the American people.

When "a blind eye" was turned to the truth of the stolen 2020 election, it became clear why "An Appeal to Heaven" had become the centerpiece of our home months earlier. We would now have to turn to God as our only hope for justice. When all avenues have been exhausted and there is nowhere else to turn, we can still "appeal to heaven," which is higher and greater than any earthy court, party, or person. We can appeal to almighty God just like our forefathers did 250 years ago. They knew they did not have a real chance to win the Revolutionary War without the intervention and miraculous hand of God moving on their behalf. They were right. America is miraculous. America is exceptional because America started with a prayer dedicating our land to Jesus Christ, and a covenant was made with the living God. That covenant still remains and stands today.

Robert Hunt was chaplain of the voyage and journey that established the first successful English colony in the New World, at Jamestown, Virginia, in 1607. After a long pilgrimage of 144 days, the 105 men and boys made landfall at the mouth of the Chesapeake Bay at the Atlantic Ocean. They named the place Cape Henry after the son of King James. On April 29, 1607, Rev. Robert Hunt led a group from the expedition to a place on the beach where they had erected a cross. Hunt led the group in a prayer that would forever mark and influence the future of the nation and people that would follow. Today, Cape Henry is located in Virginia Beach, Virginia.

This was the prayer[8]:

8   "Robert Hunt (chaplain)," Wikipedia, last modified August 12, 2021, https://en.wikipedia.org/wiki/Robert_Hunt_(chaplain).

We do hereby dedicate this Land, and ourselves, to reach the People within these shores with the Gospel of Jesus Christ, and to raise up Godly generations after us, and with these generations take the Kingdom of God to all the earth. May this Covenant of Dedication remain to all generations, as long as this earth remains, and may this Land, along with England, be Evangelist to the World. May all who see this Cross, remember what we have done here, and may those who come here to inhabit join us in this Covenant and in this most noble work that the Holy Scriptures may be fulfilled.

—Robert Hunt, 1607[9]

This is the proof that America is a Christian nation. From its inception, America was dedicated to Jesus Christ, and it was America's Christian foundation that was the centerpiece in the footing of the American Revolution that came over 150 years later.

I cannot help but think of Thomas Paine's *Common Sense*. If we ever needed common sense, it is now. This forty-seven-page pamphlet was authored by Paine in 1775–1776 and written to the people of the thirteen original colonies. It advocated independence from Great Britain and used moral and political arguments to encourage the colonists to fight for their freedom. It was an instant sensation and success, and it had the largest sale and circulation of any book published in American history. *Common Sense* made a convincing and passionate case for independence and was written and structured as if it were a sermon.[10]

9   Gary Demar, "Choose You this Day Whose Notes You Will Follow," last modified August 19, 2008, https://americanvision.org/1644/choose-day-whose-notes-will-follow/.
10   "Thomas Paine," Wikipedia, last modified November 24, 2021, www.wikipedia.org/wiki/Thomas_Paine.

The First Great Awakening was also wrapping up around this time. Also known as the "Great Awakening," it was a series of Christian revivals that swept the thirteen colonies as well as England, Scotland, and Germany in the 1730s–1770s. Tens of thousands of non-religious colonists were converted to Protestant beliefs, which had an immense impact on church attendance, homes, workplaces, entertainment, and colleges. The moral climate of the colonies was greatly altered due to the Great Awakening, and this helped to encourage the Revolutionary movement. It is widely accepted that the First Great Awakening paved the way for independence. Indeed, America was born out of revival.[11]

I was led to do my own research on my family heritage and look back into my lineage. My maiden name is French, and while I grew up hearing a lot of stories about my ancestry, I felt the Lord was asking me to do my own research. What I found was incredible. I am the direct descendent of a French Huguenot. You may be asking, "What is that?" I did not know what that was myself until I did my own inquiry.

In short, French Huguenots were French Protestants. The Protestant Reformation reached France in the early 1600s, and the Huguenot Church in France was growing quickly; however, 90 percent of France was still Roman Catholic, and the Catholic Church was intent on remaining in control. These Protestant believers fled France under extreme persecution and great threats of death to find freedom in the New World. The mass exodus began in the early part of the 1600s and lasted through the late 1700s.[12]

---

11   "First Great Awakening," Wikipedia, last modified November 28, 2021, www.wikipedia.org/wiki/First_Great_Awakening.
12   "Huguenot History," The Huguenot Society of America, https://www.huguenotsocietyofamerica.org/history/huguenot-history/.

Huguenot pioneers resettled to the American colonies directly from France and indirectly from the Protestant countries of Europe.

They made their new homes up and down the coast of North America, but the states of Massachusetts, New York, Pennsylvania, Virginia, and South Carolina held the largest populations of Huguenots. These colonists became part of the fabric that was being woven into the beautiful tapestry that would become America. George Washington was the grandson of a Huguenot on his mother's side as well as Paul Revere, whose father was a Huguenot.[13]

Please allow me to paint a picture here. These Huguenots were not "casual Christians." They had been brutally slaughtered, targeted, and labeled as "heretics." Many had their homes and possessions taken or were ordered to renounce their faith and join the Catholic Church. Instead of renouncing their faith and "falling into line," these passionate Christians chose to leave everything they knew to find a life where they could worship freely. Just the journey across the Atlantic could often be deadly, but these pioneers braved the journey and a completely unknown and foreign existence in a new world for their faith and their families. These were dedicated and impassioned Christians who had to be deeply sincere and devout in their faith.

My eighth great-grandfather, Antoine Poitevin, was born in 1640 in France and arrived with his wife, Gabrielle Berou Poitevin, and their two sons and one daughter, sometime around 1682 or earlier. They settled in what would later become Charleston, South Carolina. A known haven at the time for French Huguenots. I was deeply humbled and moved with intense emotion to discover my true natural lineage is that of a devout Christian pioneer and believer. It felt as if the pieces of the puzzle were finally coming together.[14]

13   "Huguenot History," The Huguenot Society of America, https://www.huguenotsocietyofamerica.org/history/huguenot-history/.
14   Ancestry, www.ancestry.com/family-tree/AntoinePoitevin.

I remember quite vividly having many questions after my "Damascus Road" experience and dramatic conversion back at the farm. That's where it all began so many years earlier, and I had a lot of time there by myself, and I did a lot of thinking. I began to look back at my life and wonder, *Where were the signposts or flags in my life that anything like this would happen to me?* Later, as I grew in my faith, I began to wonder who was praying for me that this kind of dramatic intervention would or could take place in my life. I was aware of the power of prayer, and I knew the Lord worked through prayer, so I began to ask the Lord who was praying for me. I had people I knew that were born-again Christians, but I did not have any born-again Christians in my direct family at that time. I always thought I was a "first-generation born-again Christian." I knew the loneliness of that role well, but I was also a pioneer, and I was learning to walk that out.

Now, finally, I had the truth. I was not actually a "first-generation Christian"; I came from a line of devout, passionate believers who fought and stood for their faith—even in the face of death. The Bible says in Exodus 20:5 that there is a blessing that travels down a thousand generations of those who love the Lord and obey Him.

"But I lavish unfailing love for a thousand generations on those who love me and obey my commands" (Exodus 20:6, NLT).

I think I found my answer. The blessing that was on my forefathers had found its way to me in my generation. "...for such a time as this..." (Esther 4:14, KJV). I am also reminded of Hebrews 12 and "the great cloud of witnesses" that is watching us from heaven. The saints of old are there, and I know my family in the faith that went before me is a part of this "great cloud" watching us as well.

> As for us, we have all of these great witnesses who encircle us like clouds. So we must let go of every wound that has pierced us and the sin we do easily fall into. Then we

will be able to run life's marathon race with passion and determination, for the path has been already marked out before us.

Hebrews 12:1 (TPT)

This "great cloud of witnesses" mentioned in Hebrews 12 is looking down on us, and while they have run their race and are now in glory, I believe they are also watching us as we run ours. Let us run our race well.

When I look back on my life, I see two lives—before Christ and after Christ. Meeting Jesus Christ has and always will be the defining moment in my life. Nothing has been the same since I met Him on a dark and lonely night at a farm in rural Georgia. He's also changed my perspective on my past, as nothing in my former life looks the same. This should come as no surprise as He says in Revelation 21:5 (NIV), "...I am making everything new!" Who else but the One who created it all could also make all things new?

Reflecting on my life before Christ, I can also see a crisis in identity. I had no idea who I really was or what I was created to be. Today, I see myself as a totally new person—a new creation in Christ (2 Corinthians 5:17). I received a new start when I received a new heart. We see this clearly in Ezekiel 11.

"Then I will sprinkle clean water on you, and you will be clean. Your filth will be washed away, and you will no longer worship idols. And I will give you a new heart, and I will put a new spirit in you. I will take out your stony, stubborn heart and give you a tender, responsive heart.

And I will put my Spirit in you so that you will follow my decrees and be careful to obey my regulations."

Ezekiel 36:25–27 (NLT)

When I look at America today, I see the same crisis in identity. America was God's idea, and her identity is lost without Christ in the center of it all. America is supposed to be a city shining on a hill for all the world to see. We, as born-again Christians, are supposed to be the light of America. We can see this in the gospel of Matthew.

> "Your lives are like salt among the people. But if you, like salt, become bland, how can your 'saltiness' be restored? Flavorless salt is good for nothing and will be thrown out and trampled on by others. Your lives light up the world. For how can you hide a city that stands on a hilltop? And who would light a lamp and then hide it in an obscure place? Instead it's placed where everyone in the house can benefit from its light. So don't hide your light! Let it shine brightly before others, so that your commendable works will shine as light upon them, and then they will give their praise to your Father in heaven."

Matthew 5:13–16 (TPT)

My ancestors fled France with the light of the gospel burning in their hearts, and they brought that light here. The pilgrims we celebrate every Thanksgiving came to the New World under the same threat of death and persecution as the Huguenots, and they were carriers of this light as well. These pilgrims were also pioneers of the gospel. Today, the Lord is calling us to steward that light well and not let it be extinguished in this present evil age (Galatians 1:4). That same light burns in my heart today. It's this fire that changes lives, families, nations, and the world. Yes, it is dangerous to many because so many have made themselves enemies to the living God, but to us who are being saved, it is the power of God (1 Corinthians 1:18).

> To preach the message of the cross seems like sheer nonsense to those who are on their way to destruction, but to us who are being saved, it is the mighty power of God released within us. For it is written: I will dismantle the wisdom of the wise and I will invalidate the intelligence of the scholars. So where is the wise philosopher who understands? Where is the expert scholar who comprehends? And where is the willed debater of our time who could win a debate with God? Hasn't God demonstrated that the wisdom of this world system is utter foolishness? For in his wisdom, God designed that all the world's wisdom would be insufficient to lead people to the discovery of himself. He took great delight in baffling the wisdom of the world by using the simplicity of preaching the story of the cross in order to save those who believe it. For the Jews constantly demand to see miraculous signs, while those who are not Jews constantly cling to the world's wisdom, but we preach the crucified Messiah. The Jews stumble over him and the rest of the world sees him as foolishness. But for those who have been chosen to follow him, both Jews and Greeks, he is God's mighty power, God's true wisdom, and our Messiah.

> 1 Corinthians 1:18–24 (TPT)

I believe the church of Jesus Christ is being mobilized right now to do the impossible and that America shall be saved. Our children and our children's children are depending on us to answer the call in our generation—to be the one. We are not accountable for what took place during the reformation or the revolution, but we will be held accountable for what we do with our lives now. This can be our finest hour and our defining moment. The Lord woke me up on January 31, 2021, at 11:30 pm and told me we were entering "The Decade of Difference." I was filled with great hope and expectancy when I heard this word being spoken to me by the Spirit of the Lord. Despite everything that may look contrary in the natural, I believe we have entered a period of great change, and America's best days are still ahead of her. Let us press on in faith and receive the heavenly prize waiting for each of us in Christ (Philippians 3:14).

Please pray with me.

Father, we thank You for America. It was and still is Your idea. America is exceptional, and America is miraculous. As we face insurmountable odds and obstacles on every front, help us to not cower and shrink back in fear. Help us to be as bold as lions and as innocent as doves (Matthew 10:16). Help us to remember who we are in You and know that we can always "appeal to heaven." Father, we pray for those who are lost and do not know who they really are. We pray for their identity crisis to come to an abrupt end. We pray for the grace to surrender to Your perfect will and Your way in their lives. Father, we also pray for America to return to You and find her rightful identity in You as well. We know that You take covenants very seriously, and the covenant that was established at Cape Henry in 1607 has not been forgotten and still stands today. We pray and believe that America will return to her roots and regain her role as a city shining on a hill. We pray for the complete abolition of abortion in America and that the example

America sets in abolishing abortion will set the stage for abortion being banned across the globe. We pray for the billion-soul harvest and the fullness of the last great awakening that has already begun. Father, we know You are giving Your sons and daughters specific assignments in these last final days. We pray that Your kids will take the baton and run their race well. We know that the saints who have gone before us are cheering us on (Hebrews 12:1), and we know that Jesus Christ is always interceding for us (Hebrews 7:25). We have nothing to fear (Isaiah 41:10), and those who are with us are more than those against us (2 Kings 6:16). Lord, help us to answer the call on each of our lives and embrace that call and our destiny in Christ fully. We know that many have been brought into Your Kingdom for such a time as this (Ester 4:14). Finally, we want to pray for the children. These are Your precious ones, and we thank You for Your angelic ministry in each and every one of their lives. We thank You for their protection and that they are safe in the shelter of Your wings (Psalm 91:4). We also pray for the overturning of every single piece of immoral and unrighteous legislation that has been loosed from hell with the intent to destroy the next generation. Thank You for raising up righteous leaders who fear God more than anything else and are willing to fight the good fight of faith in every mountain of influence. Father, we know that all this is impossible on our own, but we know it is not impossible with You. You are the God of the impossible (Luke 1:37). Finally, Father, we thank You for snatching others from the fire of destruction just like You rescued me so many years ago. Father, thank You for rescuing Your chosen ones from the devourer. We pray that not one will be lost, but all will be saved (2 Peter 3:9). We pray this in the mighty name above all names—the name of Jesus Christ, our Lord and Savior. Amen.

Epilogue

Since completing the original manuscript for what would become *In the Company of Saints and Sinners*, I continued to see the hand of God at work. Before I ever typed a single word of the book, I had a dream where I felt the Lord was speaking to me to use TBN to publish my book. I had to get up and go on the internet to find out if TBN even published books. To my surprise, I found Trilogy Publishing as part of the TBN family. I began writing the manuscript shortly after.

When I finished writing, I began to pray about the next steps. I kept coming back to the dream I had of TBN publishing my book. I reached out to Trilogy Publishing and spoke with a representative and began to seriously pray about submitting my manuscript for consideration. I submitted my manuscript about a week later, and on October 27, 2021, my manuscript was accepted, and I was issued a publishing contract with Trilogy Publishing.

October 27, 2021, is the fifteenth anniversary of the "day my life changed forever." I go into great detail about that day in this book, and for about a decade, I referred to October 27, 2006, as the "worst day of my life." I went to work as a lobbyist like any other day, and by the end of the day, my life looked and felt like it was over. I don't call it the "worst day of my life" now. It was the day that everything changed forever. It was the beginning of the end, and the result was my conversion to Christ.

How fitting that the Lord would use a day I equated with disgrace and contempt and fifteen years later turn it around to make it a day of redemption. A day that was designed to destroy me is now a day of restoration. The story the devourer wrote to devour me is now a story the Lord has rewritten for His glory. Hallelujah.

About the Author

Catherine Butte is a graduate of the University of Georgia and Charis Bible College in Woodland Park, Colorado. Her testimony has aired on national television as well as worldwide media. She and her husband, Aaron, live in Virginia Beach, Virginia, with their two sons, Daniel and David.